AF541161

DUAL ROLE OF WOMEN IN BANKING SECTOR

DUAL ROLE OF WOMEN IN BANKING SECTOR

By

Dr. S.N.Brintha

M.Com, M.Phil, Ph.D., MBA

Manonmaniam Sundaranar University

Tirunelveli (Tamil Nadu)

(India)

&

Dr. X. Antony Thanaraj

Associate Professor

Department of Commerce

Scott Christian College

Nagercoil (Tamil Nadu)

(India)

DISCOVERY PUBLISHING HOUSE PVT. LTD.

NEW DELHI-110 002

Published by:
Tilak Wasan

DISCOVERY PUBLISHING HOUSE PVT. LTD.
4383/4B, Ansari Road, Darya Ganj
New Delhi-110 002 (India)
Phone : +91-11-23279245, 43596064-65
Fax : +91-11-23253475
E-mail : discoverypublishinghouse@gmail.com
sales@discoverypublishinggroup.com
parul.wasan@gmail.com
web : www.discoverypublishinggroup.com

***First Edition:* 2014**

ISBN: 978-93-5056-414-1

Dual Role of Women in Banking Sector

Printed at:
Dynamic Printers
Delhi

Preface

Men and Women are alike in that they both strive to strike a Work-life balance. However, the equations at work place for each of them vary. This becomes more evident especially in case of women who have responsibilities at home (they could be married or unmarried). For women it is a constant struggle to create the perfect expected image at work and at home.

At work, women employees are often compared to their male counterparts. Now, if the comparison is for work performance and quality, it's perfectly fair. However, when Women are indirectly or directly pressurized to work long hours to prove their commitment towards their job, it's rather unfair, because a women working late at office is compromising on many fronts – she is probably compromising her relationship with her in-laws or her husband, may be she is neglecting her children or her personal time, health and development.

A corporate entity is a part of the larger world and as a corporate citizen companies should be held responsible towards the safety, security, health and well-being of their employees. A good management runs business on fairly fair terms. In India, we emulate western world and western culture on all fronts. However when it comes to work culture, our deep rooted Indian ethos overpower all the sophistication. We go to the extent of indianising the work culture of multi-nationals as well, who otherwise are more mindful of employee's work-life balance.

This book has covered all the major segments of the subject and is divided into seven chapters spread over the following topics – Introduction and Design of the Study, Conceptual Framework of the

Study, Profile of the Women Employees of Commercial Banks and their Social Support, Work-life Imbalance and Its Antecedents, Consequences of Work-life Imbalance, Impact of Work-life Imbalance on the Coping Strategies for Work-life Balance and Summary of Findings, Conclusion and Recommendations. I hope it would serve as a useful text and reference book for all categories of readers, particularly academics, researchers, practitioners and governments agencies.

Any constructive criticism and suggestion is always welcome.

— Authors

Contents

1 Introduction and Design of the Study

INTRODUCTION

Work-family relationships are complex and multi-dimensional. It is an important ongoing academic and social policy area that requires multi-disciplinary and multi-level investigation collaboration. Women's participation rate in employment is increasing, giving rise to the belief that equal opportunities, for women are improving. A closer inspection would suggest that such an analysis is premature. Today, almost 75 per cent of the women, work in the lowest-paid sectors, where, full-time working women are earning an average 19 per cent less per hour than equivalent men, and women in part-time work earning a staggering 41 per cent less per hour. The adjustment of work and family balance is always a problem to women since they have dual work to do.

In more recent times, banks have significantly changed their public policies about women's access to management. Career breaks and job sharing are utilised in retention strategies. Recruitment and promotion policies claim equal opportunities. It is also noted that organizations, placing a greater emphasis on development and promotion, also enhance the livelihood of women succeeding to top management. Due to the workaholic attitude among the women employees, they have more pressures to put up with, in the organization. This affects their family life also. These are not good symptoms of the economic development since there is a lack of human welfare. Hence, there is a need for coping up with strategies, especially, among the women employees.

NEED FOR THE STUDY

Work lives either enhance or detract from family lives. Our family lives can have positive or negative influence on our work attitudes, behaviours and outcomes. For example, extensive and inflexible working hours, workaholic and job stress may produce distress within the family domain, withdrawal from family responsibilities and adversely affect one's overall quality of life. Similarly, extensive care-giving responsibilities and intensive involvement in family activities, can limit individual career choices and aspirations and negatively affect their work involvement, job satisfaction and intention to continue their employment. Hence, there is a need to balance their work-family lives. Since the work-life balance depends on many factors, the women employees have to consider all these aspects. Other-wise, the money earned from their work will not give them a peaceful life. In reality, many women employees do not know these aspects and also the management of work-life imbalance. Hence, the researcher has made an attempt in this study to analyse the factors, influencing work-life imbalance, existing work-life imbalance, consequences of work-life imbalance and the strategies necessary to maintain the balance.

STATEMENT OF THE PROBLEM

An organization that would like to create a family-friendly work place, must consider all inter-related components. But present work environment in banking industry is different. More importance is given to bench marking, work pressure and workload due to the introduction of automation and reduction of employees. It is creating a lot of work pressure especially, among the women employees since they are not sharing their problems with their co-workers and also due to their dual role. The child-care, elder-care, family care responsibilities also rest on the shoulders of the women employees. The work-family conflict can be time-based, strain-based or behaviour based. All these are affecting the potential source of life satisfaction and organizational performance. The intensity of work-family conflict on organizational out-come is greater than the family-work conflict. At the same time, the family-work conflicts affect the productivity of the employees. Hence, both these interferences are affecting the work and family lives, which is commonly seen in banking industry.

REVIEW OF PREVIOUS STUDIES

Work-life Imbalance in Banking Industry

Karatepe *et al.* (2006)[1] found that work-family imbalance increased emotional exhaustion and decreased job satisfaction among the frontline bank employees.

Netemeyer *et al.* (2004)[2] identified that work-life imbalance and emotional exhaustion are the two critical variables that have adverse effects on job outcomes of front-line employees.

Siw *et al.* (2008)[3] highlighted the importance of examining the relationship between work-family interaction and burnout over time. Their findings indicated bi-directional casual paths; *i.e.*, both work-family interaction and burnout may be either predictor or consequence, causing both loss and gain spirals as proposed by Conservation of Resources (COR) theory.

Felstead *et al.* (2002)[4] revealed that lack of balance between work and non-work activities is related to reduce psychological and physical well-being of the employees.

Hyman *et al.* (2004)[5] indicated that intrusion of work demands into personal life (*e.g.,* working during the week end) was related to the reports of heightened stress and emotional exhaustion for employees.

Aycan and Eskin (2004)[6] demonstrated that organizational support as manifested by supervisory support, work-family conflict and practices, and time demand and flexibility are critical for reducing both male and female employees' work-family conflict in Turkish Retail Banks.

Spinks (2004)[7] revealed that the front line bank employees, play a critical role in delivering high quality services and creating a pool of satisfied customers. Despite this recognition, there is a lack of family-friendly policies or there are problems associated with the implementation of these policies in the retail banking environment.

Osman and Mehmet (2006)[8] revealed that work-family conflict increased emotional exhaustion and decreased job satisfaction. Intrinsic motivation was found to exert a significant negative impact on emotional exhaustion. A high level of intrinsic motivation, results in high levels of job performance, job satisfaction and affective commitment to the organization.

Yavas *et al.* (2003)[9] identified the negative influence of the work-life imbalance among the employees on their service recovery performance in banks.

Role Stressors among the Women

Davidson and Cooper (1994)[10] suggested that female managers are often confronted with additional pressures from both their homes and job environment as compared to their male counterparts.

Aditya and Sen (1993)[11] compared the level of stress between Indian men and women executives. Results showed that male and female executives differed significantly on role ambiguity, role conflict, inter-role distance, future prospects, and human relations at work, femininity, and masculine by dimensions.

Pareek and Mehta (1997)[12] studied three groups of working Indian women and the type of role stresses experienced by them. The study found that the banking employees faced with medium stress on all dimensions whereas the gazette officers were having higher stress. The school teachers were having less stress.

Daga and Husain (2001)[13] studied the relationship between social support and stress. Social support acted as a buffer against stress in all the three categories namely clerks, doctors and teachers.

Aziz (2003)[14] investigated the prevalence of organizational role stress among Indian information technology employees. Resource inadequacy emerged as the most potent stress factor. The study reported more stress among men as compared to women.

Work-family Conflict

Howard *et al.* (2004)[15] found that work-family conflict, when duties affect one's ability to meet family responsibilities, is far more important in determining an employee's job satisfaction than family-work conflict, which occurs when attending to family responsibilities making it more difficult to accomplish work-related tasks.

Powell and Jeffrey (2006)[16] found that the role segmentations may diminish the extent of both Work-Family Enrichment (WFE) and Work-Family conflict (WFC) whereas role integration may increase the likehood of both WFE and WFC. The relationships between WFC and WFE have led to the conclusion that WFC and WFE are independent and unrelated constructs.

Family-work Conflict

Williams and Alliger (1994)[17] identified that the inter-domain conflict between work and home domains has become a major concern for employees due to the conflict generated in facilities as work intrudes into family life and vice-versa. The multiple time and task requirements faced by employees, as they juggle work, and family responsibilities can create conflicts and the conflict between the work and family domain is of increasing concern in today's organizational environment.

Kossek and Ozeki (1998)[18] suggested that work-family conflict has negative consequences and has been linked with work place perceptions and attitudes. Inter-domain conflict seems to occur with front-line, blue-collar, employees, business owners, professionals and managers.

Antecedents of Work-family Conflict

Mainiero and Sullivan (2005)[19] revealed that organizations concerned about improving their cultures for work-family balance, have much to gain in terms of reduced burnout and absenteeism and increased job satisfaction, commitment and performance.

Peters *et al.* (2005)[20] explained the importance of role of gender in the relationship between conflicts in the work-family interface, emotional exhaustion and job outcomes.

Moncrief, *et al.* (2002)[21] mentioned that an understanding of the presence of male-female differences in the relationship between inter-role conflicts, emotional exhaustion, job performance and turnover intention is crucial for managers in determining if an undifferentiated or dual approach is warranted in managing frontline employees.

Wayne *et al.* (2004)[22] found that women value more and assign a higher priority to their family roles than their work roles. On the other hand, men attach higher priorities to their job-related responsibilities. In an era of excessive job demands, irregular and incompatible schedules, and long work hours, women employees experience greater family-work conflict due to be the higher priority they place on family roles.

Posig and Kickul (2004)[23] revealed that the relationship between family-work conflict and emotional exhaustion was stronger among female employees compared with male employees.

Demerouti *et al.* (2005)[24] demonstrated that the relationship between partner's rating of work-family conflict and exhaustion was higher among women than men.

Martuis *et al.* (2002)[25] identified that there is a distinction between the two sexes' like the type of things each gender values, in various aspects of their lives, including their jobs. Accordingly, one would expect inter-role conflicts to affect the job performances of relationship-valuing female employees, more negatively in interactions-oriented frontline jobs where employees are expected to deal with customer requests and complaints through long work hours.

Kinman *et al.* (2006)[26] identified that the most stressful aspects of academic and academic-related works to be long working hours, too much administrative paper work, lack of support, obtaining research funding and finding time for research, frequent interruptions, rapid change, poor leadership and management, poor salary and lack of promotion prospects.

Gomez, (2004)[27] revealed that the socio-demographic characteristic that may influence the work-family conflict is the level of education. The training and education level of some employees may reinforce their role as moving away from family and increasing their commitment to the organization. Highly-educated employees may have more opportunities to get promoted or move geographically to another organization site.

Impact of Work-family Conflict

Elloy and Smith (2003)[28] revealed that dual-career couples may have needs that are different from those of more traditional single-career couple. In the work environment, dual-career employees' status implies the need for greater employee sensitivity and awareness of the conflicting demands for simultaneous careers, so that employees may become more effective both at work and at home.

Siegal *et al.* (2005)[29] reported that perception of organizational justice can moderate the impact of work-family conflict upon employees' organizational commitment. Thus, if the procedures by which work hours, rosters, work load and access to work-life supports are made available are perceived to be fair. Then work-family conflict experienced is less likely to result in negative feelings towards the project.

Coping Strategies and Work-life Balance

Wilson, *et al.* (2007)[30] concluded that the inclusion of social coping strategies, combined with family involvement, significantly reduced work-family conflict. Open response categories on the survey suggest that these reductions were due to the facilitation of a joint problem-solving approach by family members. In contrast, employee-focused training on psychological coping alone appears to increase family conflicts.

Rotondo, *et al.* (2003)[31] identified that both time-based conflict and strain-based conflicts were lower among persons employing direct action coping at home. Direct action-coping involves individually-motivated effort towards the resolution of family problems that may cause work to suffer. This coping style reflects the tendency to tackle the problems and do what needs to be done within family domains so that conflict is reduced.

Carman and Shaffer (2001)[32] pointed out that the parental demands and hours spent on household work were a significant predictor of behaviour-based family interference with work (FIW). The role-stressor variables and hours spent on paid work were the significant determinants of work interference with family (WIF). Gender was an important predicator of both FIW and WIF.

Promotion of Work-life Balance

Francis (2005)[33] identified the importance of a supportive work environment in promoting employees' work-life balance. Managerial support was seen as a critical factor in facilitating work-life balance in the case study project, as managers and supervisors often act as 'gatekeepers' for access to work-life policies. Achievement of the health and well-being key-result areas led to the implementation of work-life intervention such as roistered days off for salaried staff and flexible working hours which positively influence the employees work-life balance.

Casper *et al.* (2007)[34] suggested that organizations can enhance positive outcome by providing work-life programmes that appeal to a wider array of employees. Employees' needs vary according to gender, age, and stage of family development. Furthermore, it would be expected that employees' needs will change over time and this will be influenced by the changing nature of roles and responsibilities that employees take in their personal lives.

Hamilton, *et al.* (2006)[35] revealed that single and child-free workers do not have access to resources, that can help alleviate work-life conflicts arguably exacerbating, rather than reducing their experienced conflict.

Saltzstein *et al.* (2001)[36] mentioned that work-based social support is positively related to job satisfaction directly and through work-family conflict as a mediating variable. The family-friendly polities at work may decrease work-family conflict, improving work-family balance and, in turn, job satisfaction.

Gordon and Whelan (2004)[37] found that the work-based and personal social supports are associated with work-family balance. In addition, work-based social support was associated with all of the work outcomes tested, and personal social support was associated with job satisfaction and organizational commitment.

Posig and Kickul (2004)[38] found a significant relationship between work-family conflict and family-work conflict for females but not for males. For male employees, work-family conflict mediates the relationship between work-role expectation and emotional exhaustions. For female employees, work-family conflict, family-work conflict, and work-role expectations were significant. Emotional exhaustion is directly influenced by work-role expectation as well as by work-family conflict.

Lee and Choo (2001)[39] identified the need for greater spouse support, flexible work schedule, and full-day school, in order to alleviate work-family conflict. Maintenance of good material relations is important in reducing spouse conflict and increasing well-being in women entrepreneurs.

Hanebuth *et al.* (2006)[40] have related effort-reward in balance to serious outcomes such as psychosomatic symptomatology sleep disturbances, fatigue, problem, alcohol consumption, absenteeism and turnover.

Fahlen (2006)[41] identified that employees who are more over-committed to work show poorer physical and psychological health.

Research Gap

The above said review of previous studies discussed the work-life conflict, its causes and consequences and the coping strategies adopted by the employees to maintain the work-life balance. All these studies have been undertaken only in foreign countries. Though work-life imbalance and work-life conflict have been studied by a few in the Indian context, there is no exclusive study on work-family conflict and family-work conflicts, its antecedents and outcomes in banking industry. Hence the researcher in the present study has made an attempt to fill up the research gap. A research model has been proposed to fillup the research gap.

Proposed Research Model

The proposed research model is shown in Figure 1.1.

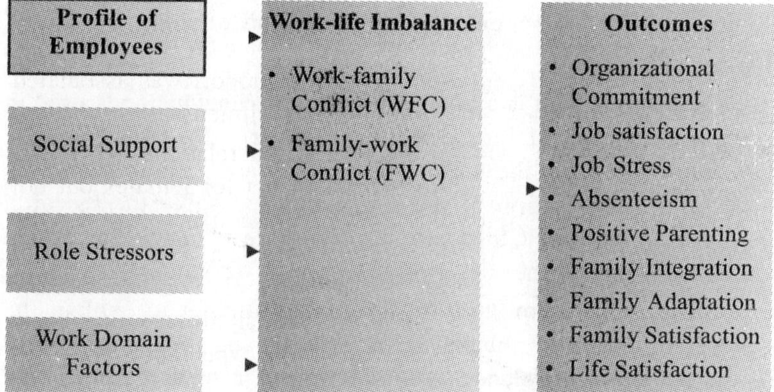

Fig. 1.1: Proposed Research Model

OBJECTIVES OF THE STUDY

Based on the proposed research model, the objectives of the study are

(i) To exhibit the socio-economic profile and social support of the employees

(ii) To analyse the important antecedents of work-life imbalance among the employees

(iii) To measure the work-life imbalance (Work-Family Conflict and Family-Work Conflict) among the employees

(iv) To analyse the association between the profile, social support of the employees and their work-life imbalance

(v) To examine the various outcomes of work-life imbalance

(vi) To evaluate the impact of work-life imbalance on the various outcomes of work-life imbalance and

(vii) To analyse the level of implementation of coping strategies and its impact on the work-life imbalance among the employees.

RESEARCH METHODOLOGY

Research Methodology enlightens the methods to be followed in research works starting from investigation to presentation of research report. The research methodology focuses on the methods to be adopted at various levels of the research process. It includes research design, area of the study, population of the study, sampling design, sources of data, collection of data and analysis of data.

Research Design

Research design is a blue print of the various methods used in research projects. It includes the procedures for obtaining the information needed, the way in which they are processed and the method of presentation of the suggestions to solve the research problems. Eventhough, the research designs are too many, the present study has followed the 'descriptive' research design.

Since the present study has made an attempt to explain the concept of work-life imbalance, the reasons and the consequences of the work-life imbalance, it is descriptive in nature. Apart from this, the present study has its own objectives and methodology to fulfill the objectives of the study, and hence it is 'descriptive in nature'. Since, the study also focuses on the cause and effect, the relationship between the antecedents of work-life imbalance (WLI), impact of WLI on its various outcomes and the impact of implementation of coping strategies on the WLI, it is also diagnostic in nature. Hence the applied research design of the study is descriptive and diagnostic in nature.

Area of the Study

It is imperative to select the area of the study since the concept of work-life imbalance is found in almost all fields in the economy. Nowadays, women employment is growing in all sectors of the Indian Economy. Even though, it may increase the national and percapita income of the nation, the welfare of the women employees is affected because of their work-life imbalance. Hence, the present study focuses on this area. The selected field of the research is commercial banking since the banking industry has been facing rapid changes, especially, after globalization. The area of the study is confined to Kanyakumari district because of the researcher's nativity.

Selection of the Study Area

Kanyakumari district was purposively selected as the study area by the researcher for the following reasons.

1. There is no exclusive study made on the work-life imbalance among the women employees in Kanyakumari district.
2. The commercial banks are providing more opportunities to the women employees in their banks.
3. The district has a highly educated population and the number of employed couples is higher in the district.
4. Familiarity to culture, local dialect and infrastructure facilities would help the researcher to develop a good rapport with the Human Relation. Manager and also the staff working in the various branches of banks at the district.

Population of the District

The total number of bank branches in urban, semi-urban and rural areas of the district during 2009-10 has been collected from the lead bank office of the district. The number of public, private and co-operative bank branches in the study area is shown in Table 1.1.

Table: 1.1: Number of branches of various banks in kanyakumari district

Sl.No.	Sector	Number of Branches in			Total
		Urban	Sub-urban	Rural	
1.	Public	33	71	13	117
2.	Private	12	15	7	34
3.	Co-operative	7	16	1	24
	Total	**52**	**102**	**21**	**175**

Source: annual credit plan, lead bank office, nagercoil.

Out of the 175 bank branches in the district, 66.86 per cent of the branches belong to Public Sector whereas 19.43 per cent belong to private sector. The remaining 13.71 per cent of the bank branches are co-operative banks. In total, a maximum of 58.29 per cent of the bank branches are in sub-urban area, followed by 29.71 per cent of the bank branches situated in urban areas. The remaining 12 per cent is at rural areas.

Number of Bank Employees in the District

The total number of bank employees has been collected from the various branches of the district. The bank employees are classified into three important categories namely managers and supervisors, clerks and cashiers and sub staff. The distribution of bank employees on the basis of their categories in public, private and co-operative banks is summarized in Table 1.2.

Table: 1.2: Number of bank employees in kanyakumari district

Sl.No.	Sector of the Bank	Number of Employees			Total
		Urban	Sub-urban	Rural	
1.	Public	308	509	303	1120
2.	Private	96	181	104	381
3.	Co-operative	54	103	46	203
	Total	**458**	**793**	**453**	**1704**

Source: Records of bank branches in kanyakumari district

Totally, 1704 employees are working in banks in the district. Out of the 1704 employees, 46.54 per cent are clerks and cashiers, 26.88 per cent are managers and assistant manager. The remaining 26.58 per cent are sub-staff. The numbers of employees working in public sector banks constitute 65.73 per cent to the total. It is followed by 22.36 per cent of the employees working in private sector banks. The remaining 11.91 per cent are employed in co-operative banks.

Number of Women Employees in Banks in Kanyakumari District

The number of women employees working in the public, private and co-operative banks during 2009 has been collected from the records of all bank branches of the district and given in Table 1.3.

Out of 1704 employees, 34.57 per cent are women employees. The numbers of women employees working in public, private and co-operative banks are 399, 159 and 31 employees respectively.

Table: 1.3: Number of women employees in banks

Sl. No.	Sector of the Bank	Number of Employees			Total
		Managers and Assistant Manager	Clerks and Cashiers	Sub-staff	
1.	Public	89	284	26	399
2.	Private	38	114	7	159
3.	Co-operative	4	21	6	31
	Total	**131**	**419**	**39**	**589**

Source: Records of bank branches in Kanyakumari district

The number of female staff (clerks and cashiers) working in banks constitute 71.14 per cent of the total. Which is followed by managers and assistant manager with 22.24 per cent to its total. The number of female sub-staff working in banks is 39.

Sampling Framework of the Study

The census study has been followed to identify the samples of the present study. The co-operative banks are not included in the present study, and the female sub-staff working in public and private sector banks have also been excluded from the study. The number of female employees [Managers and assistant Manager; and Clerks and Cashiers (Staff)] working in public and private sector banks in the district have been included in the present study. The numbers of female employees working in public and private sector banks selected for the study are 373 and 152 respectively. The total employees of 525 have been selected samples for the present study. Hence, the applied sampling procedure is 'census method'. Out of 525 sample employees, the fully responded employees are only 421. Since the response rate is 80.19 per cent. Hence, 421 have been included as the sample for the present study.

Collection of Data

The required data for the present study is collected with the help of interview schedule. The schedule has been divided into four important parts. The first part covers the profile of the employees and their social support whereas the second part includes the antecedents of work-life imbalance among the employees (Role stressors and Work domain variables). The third part deals with the level of work-family conflict and family-work conflict; and the various outcomes of the work-life imbalance. The last part covers the level of implementation of coping strategies to manage the work-life balance. The related variables have been drawn from the review of previous studies and views of experts. A pilot study was conducted among 50 women employees in the commercial banks at Nagercoil town for the enrichment of the interview schedule. Certain modification, additions and deletions had been carried out to enrich the quality of the schedule.

Frame Work of Analysis

Appropriate statistical tools have been administered to analyse the data. The tools are selected on the basis of the nature of data and the objectives to be fulfilled. The applied statistical tools and the relevance of their application are summated below:

(i) T - test

The 't' test has been used to find out the significant difference among the employees in Public Sector Banks (PSBs) and Private Sector Banks (PRBs) regarding their antecedents and out comes of work-life imbalance.

(ii) One-way analysis of variance

The one way ANOVA has been administered to examine the association between the profile variables, family variables and organization variables with the social support, various aspects of work-life imbalance namely Work-family conflict, Family-work conflict and also various outcomes of work-life imbalance.

(iii) Factor analysis

The Exploratory Factor Analysis has been executed to narrate the variables related to work-life imbalance.

(iv) Confirmatory factor analysis

The Confirmatory Factor Analysis has been administered to analyse the reliability and validity of the various constructs related to antecedents and outcomes of work-life imbalance.

(v) Correlation analysis

The correlation analysis has been executed to analyse the relationship between profile variables and the work-life imbalance.

*(vi) **Regression analysis***

The regression analysis has been administered to find out the impact of work life imbalance (Work-family conflict and Family-work conflict) on the various outcomes of work-life imbalance.

The regression analysis has also been applied to analyse the impact of level of implementation of coping strategy on the work-life imbalance.

LIMITATIONS OF THE STUDY

The present study is subjected with the following limitations.

1. The present study confined its scope with women employees in PSBs and PRBs alone.
2. The variables related to the various aspects in work-life imbalance are generated with the help of previous studies and also the views of the experts.
3. The antecedents and outcomes of work life imbalance have been examined with the help of appropriate statistical tools which have their own limitation.
4. The variables related to many aspects in work-life imbalance have been measured at Likert five point scale for the uniformity and also the application of relevant statistical tools.
5. Kanyakumari district has been purposively selected for the present study. Since, the sample size is too limited, the scope of application of the findings of the present study is too limited.

SCHEME OF THE REPORT

For a neat and clear presentation of the report, the present study is classified into seven chapters.

The first chapter includes the introduction, need for the study, statement of the problem, review of previous studies, research gap, proposed research model, objectives of the study, methodology and chapterisation.

The second chapter explains the conceptual frame work of the study. It explains family domain and work domain variables, social support, work-family and family-work conflicts, organizational commitment, job satisfaction, job stress, absenteeism, positive parenting, parental satisfaction, family adaptation, family satisfaction, life satisfaction and strategy implemented by the employees.

The third chapter explains the profile of the employees control variables, family domain variables, organization variables and social support among the employees in PSBs and PRBs.

The fourth chapter covers the antecedents of work-life imbalance, organizational role stressors and work domain variables and association between the profile of employees and their perception on various antecedents of work life imbalance, the work-family conflict and family-work conflict among the employees and the impact of antecedents on work life imbalance.

The fifth chapter explains the various consequences of the work-life imbalance namely organizational commitment, job satisfaction, job stress, absentisim, positive parenting, family integration, parental satisfaction, family adaptation, family satisfaction and life satisfaction among the employees.

The sixth chapter includes the impact of work-life imbalance (WFC and FWC) on various outcomes, impact of social support on implementation of coping strategies and impact of implementation of coping strategies on work-life imbalance.

The seventh chapter reveals the summary of the findings of the study, conclusion, suggestions and also the scope of further research.

References

1. Karatepe, O. and Tekinkus, M. (2006), "The Effects of Work-family Conflict, Emotional Exhaustion, and Intrinsic Motivation on Job Outcomes of Front-line Employees", *International Journal of Bank Marketing,* 24(3): 173-193.
2. Netemeyer, R.G., Brashear-Alejandro, T. and Boles, J.S. (2004), "A cross-National Model of Job-Related Outcomes of Work Role and Family Role Variables: A Retail Banking Context", *Journal of the Academy for Marketing Science,* 32(1): 49-60.
3. Siw, Tone Instranda, Ellen Melbye Langballe, Geir Ariel Espues, Erik Falkum and Olaf Gjerlw Aasland (2008), "Positive and Negative Work-family Interaction and Burnout: A Longitudinal Study of Reciprocal Relations", *Work and Stress,* 22(1): 1-15.
4. Felstead, A., Jewson, N., Phizacklea, A. and Walter, S. (2002), "Opportunities to Work at Home in the Context of Work-life Balance," *Human Resource Management Journal,* 12(1): 54-76.
5. Hyman, J. and Summers, J. (2004), "Lacking Balance? Work-life Employment Practices in the Modern Economy", *Personal Review*, 33(4): 418-429.

6. Aycan, Z., and Eskin, M., (2004), "*Relative Contribution of Childcare, Spousal, and Organizational Support in Reducing Work-family Conflict for Males and Females: The Case of Turkey*", Paper Presented at the Academy of Management Meeting, New Orleans LA.
7. Spinks, N (2004), "Work-life Balance: Achievable Goal or Pipe Dream?" *The Journal for Quality and Participation*, 27(Fall): 4-11.
8. Osman M. Karatepe and Mehmet Tekinkus, (2006), "The Effects of Work-family Conflict, Emotional Exhaustion, and Intrinsic Motivation on Job Outcomes of Front-line Employees", *International Journal of bank Marketing,* 24(3): 173-193.
9. Yavas, U., Karaptepe, O.M, Arai, T., and Tekinus, M., (2003), "Antecedents and Outcomes of Service Recovery Performance: An Empirical Study of Frontline Employees in Turkish Banks", *International Journal of Bank Marketing,* 21(5): 255-265.
10. Davidson, M and Cooper, C., (1994), "*Shattering the Glass Ceiling*", Paul Chapman, London.
11. Aditya, S.M. and Sen, Aik (1993), "Executives Gender Stress: A Comparison between Men and Women", *Journal of the Indian Academy of Applied Psychology,* 19(1p2): 1-6.
12. Pareek, A and Mehta, M., (1997), *Role Stress among Working Women*, in Pestonjee, D.M and Pareek, V, (Eds), "Studies in Organizational Role Stress and Coping", Rawat Publications, Jaipur, pp. 173-181.
13. Daga, N and Husain, A. (2001), A Study of Social Family Role Stress and Social Support among Working Women, in Husain, A (Ed), Stress Research and Stress Management, Aligarh Muslim University, Aligarh, pp. 59-76.
14. Aziz, M., (2003), "Organizational Role Stress Among Indian Information Technology Professionals", *Asian–Pacific Newsletter on Occupational Health and Safety*, 10(2): 31-33.
15. Howard, W.G., Donoflio, N.H., and Boles, J.S. (2004), "Inter-domain Work-family, Family-work Conflict and Polices Work Satisfaction", *An International Journal of Police Strategies and Management,* 27(3): 380-395.
16. Gary N., Powell and Jeffrey H. Greenhaus (2006), "Is the Opposite of Positive Negative?", *Career Development International,* 11(7): 650-659.
17. Williams, K.J. and Alliger, G.M. (1994), "Role Stressors, Mood Spillover, and Perceptions of Work-family Conflict in Employed Parents", *Academy of Management Journal,* 37(4): 837-868.
18. Kossek, E.E., and Ozeki, C. (1998), "Work-family Conflict, Policies, and the Job-life Relationship" *A Review and Direction for Organizational Behaviour*, 33(6): 17-29.
19. Mainiero, C.A., and Sullivan, S.E., (2005), "Kaleidoscope Careers: An Alternative Explanation for the up-out Revolution", *Academy of Management Executive,* 19(1): 106-123.

20. Peters, M.C.V., Montgomery, A.J., Bakker, A. Bard Schaufeli, W.B. (2005), "Balancing Work and Home: How Job and Home Demands are Related to Turnout", *International Journal of Stress Management,* 12 (1): 43-61.

21. Moncrief, W.C., Babakus, E., Cravens, D.W and Johnson, M.W. (2002), "Examining Gender Differences in Field Sales Organization", *Journal of Business Research,* 49(3): 245-257.

22. Wayne, J.H., Musisca N., and Fleeson W. (2004), "Considering the Role of Personality in the Work-family Experience Relationships of the Big Fire to Personality in the Work-family Conflict and Facilitation", *Journal of Vocational Behaviours,* 64(1): 108-130.

23. Posig, M. and Kickul, J. (2004), "Work-role Expectations and Work-family Conflict Gender Differences in Emotional Exhaustion", *Human in Management Review,* 19(7): 373-386.

24. Demerouti, E., Baskker, R.B. and Schaufeli, W.B. (2005), "Spillover and Crossover of Exhaustion and Life Satisfaction among Dual-earner Ponents", *Journal of Vocational Behaviour,* 67(2): 266-289.

25. Martuis, L.C., Eddleston, K.A. and Vegia, J.F. (2002), "Moderators of the Relationship between Work-family Conflict and Career Satisfaction", *Academy of Management Journal,* 45(2): 399-409.

26. Kinman, G. Jones, F, and Kinman, R. (2006), "The Well being of the UK Academy: 1998 to 2004", *Quality in Higher Education,* 12(1): 15-27.

27. Gomez, S. (2004), *"La Incorporation de la Mujer al Mercado Laboral: Impacts Social Y Medidas Estructurales"*, Research Paper, IESE, Barcelona.

28. David F. Elloy and Catherine R. Smith (2003), "Patterns of Stress, Work-family Conflict, Role Conflict, Role Antiquity and Overload among Dual-career and Single-career Couples: An Australian Study", *Cross Culture Management,* 10(1): 55-63.

29. Siegal, P.A., Brockner, J., Fishman, A.Y., Hardan, C. (2005), "The Moderating Influence of Procedural Fairness on the Relationship between Work-life Conflict and Organizational Commitment", *Journal of Applied Psychology,* 90(10): 13-24.

30. Marie Gee Wilson, A. P. Debruyne, Sophie Chen and Sonia Fernandes (2007), "Shift Work Intervention for Reduced Work-family Conflict", *Employee Relations,* 29(2): 162-177.

31. Rotondo, M., Dawn S. Canlson and Joel F. Kincaid (2003), "Coping with Multiple Dimensions of Work-family Conflict", *Personal Review,* 32(3): 275-296.

32. Carman K. Fu and Management A. Shaffer, (2001), "The Tug of Work and Family: Direct and Indirect Domain Specific Determinants of Work-family Conflict", *Personnel Review,* 30(5): 502-522.

33. Francis, V.E. (2005), "The Importance of Workplace Support and Flexibility for Engineers" Combining Forces-Advancing Facilities Management and

Construction through Innovation Series, Proceedings of the CIB 2005 Conference, Helsinki, Finland, Vol. I, Section IV, June, pp. 197-209.

34. Casper, W.J., Weltman, D and Kwesiga, E. (2007), "Beyond Family-friendly the Construct and Measurement of Singles Friendly Work Culture", *Journal of Vocational Behaviour,* 70(1): 418-451.

35. Hamilton, E.A., Fordon, J.K., Whelan-Berry, K.S (2006), "Understanding the Work-wise Conflict among Married Women without Children", *Women in Management Review,* 21(5): 393-415.

36. Saltzstein, A., Ring, Y and Saltzstein, G., (2001), "Work-family Balance and Job Satisfaction: the Impact of Family-friendly Polities on Attitudes of Federal Government Employees", *Public Administration Review*, 61(4): 452-467

37. Gordon, J.R and Whelan-Berry, K.S., (2004), "It Takes two to Lango: An Empirical Study of Ferceived Spouse/Partner Support for Working Women", *Women in Management Review*, 19(5): 260-273.

38. Margaret Posig and Fill Kickul (2004), "Work-role Expectations and Work-family Conflict: Gender Differences in Emotional Exhaustion", *Workers in Management Review*, 19(7): 373-386.

39. Fear Lee Siew Kuim and Choo Seow Leing (2001)", Work-family Conflict of Women Entrepreneurs in Singapore", *Women in Mangament Review*, 16(5): 204-221.

40. Hanebuth, D., Meinel, M., and Fischer, J., (2006), "Health-related Quality of Life, Psychological Work Conditions and Absenteeism in An Industrial Sample of Blue-and White-collar Employees: A Comparison of Potential Predicators", *Journal of Occupational and Environmental Medicine*, 48(1): 28-37.

41. Fahlen, G. (2006), "Effort Reward Imbalance, Sleep Disturbances and Fastigue", *International Archives of Occupational and Environmental Health*, 79(5): 371-378.

2

Conceptual Framework of the Study

INTRODUCTION

There is a vast academic literature dealing with the issue of work-life imbalance. A complete review of literature is, beyond the purview of this series of reports and counter to our primary objective which is to get easily understood and obtain relevant information on work-life imbalance from key stakeholders. This conceptual frame work incorporates both fundamental concepts from the research literature and the key insights, the researcher has gained from the 10 years of research in this area. This research is based on the idea that an individual's ability to balance work and family will be associated with family related variables, work related variables, organizational variables and also the demographic characteristics. Further, the social support among the employees has been focused. The antecedents and consequences of work-life imbalance will be associated with so many outcomes.

Finally, the coping strategies adopted by the employees to balance work and family and also the expected social support for employees to manage the work-life imbalance have been discussed. The various concepts used in the present study and the variables to measure it are discussed below:

FAMILY VARIABLES

According to Herman and Gyllstrom (1997)[1], married individuals experience more work-family conflict than the unmarried. Greenhaus *et al.* (1989)[2] proposed that the number of hours worked per week by spouse is positively associated with the conflict between work and family. Herman and Gyllstrom (1977) revealed that parents are more likely to experience work-family conflict than non-parents. Both the number of children and age of children have been found to influence work-family conflict (Bedeian *et al.,* 1988).[3] Parental demands increase with the number of children, and parents of young children experience more conflict that the parents of older children (Pleck *et al.,* 1980).[4] The hours spent on household work may also affect work-family conflict (Gutek *et al.,* 1991).[5] The present study includes the following family domain variables namely marital status, number of children, number of young children, time devoted to parents, spouse employment, hours spent on family works and parental demands.

CONTROL VARIABLES

One of the important antecedents of WFC and FWC is 'control variables' (Maricuikus *et al.*, 2007).[6] The control variables identified by Allen, (2001)[7] and Steffy and Jones (1998)[8] are age, gender, level of education, personal income and years of experience of the respondents. In the present study, the above said five control variables are included to analyse the relationship between control variables and WFC and FWC among the employees.

WORK RELATED VARIABLES

The work domain variables are the variables which are related to the working environment, inter personal relationship, work content and work culture in the industry (Lim and Hian, 1999).[9] The work domain variables lead the employees to focus on the importance attached to their work (Kang and Singh, 2004).[10] The factors identified by the researchers (Adelina, 2002; Howard, 1980[11]; Rajeshwari, 1992[12]; Summers *et al.,* 1994[13]; and Suresh and Anantharaman (2001)[14] are related to unsupportive colleagues, performance inhibitors, effort-reward imbalance, work load, lack of empowerment, continuous pressure for improved performance and conflicting demands. The variables related to the above said factors are collected from the above said reviews and are used to measure the work domain in the present study. The variables are given in Table 2.1.

Table 2.1 Work domain variables

Sl.No.	Variables
1.	My colleagues do not help me in day-to day work plan
2.	Inadequate salary
3.	Pressure on improved performance
4.	My company do not provide enough opportunities to me
5.	My colleagues do not help me in achieving the targets
6.	No authority for decision-making in day to-day affairs
7.	No balance between my talent and salary
8.	Frequent changes in company policies
9.	My colleagues are not trust worthy
10.	Dumping of heavy work-load
11.	Sharing of job with colleagues affect my own performance
12.	No proper acceptance of employees' request
13.	Poor empowerment in all aspects
14.	Monotony of repeated work
15.	My colleagues are not supportive
16.	Lack of recognition
17.	Inconvenient working hours
18.	Busy on the job activities in holidays also
19.	No standardized working hours
20.	Inadequate provision of resources to perform better
21.	Undedicated supervisors
22.	Continuous Review of work load
23.	No scope for career development
24.	Flexibility of working hours
25.	Inadequate incentives
26.	Information overload
27.	Lack of Independence
28.	No job security
29.	Poor working conditions
30.	No clear-cut duties and responsibilities

SOCIAL SUPPORT

Social support has been studied extensively in the literatures on stress and social networks (Viswesvaran *et al.*, 1999).[15] It is conceptualized as the structure of relationships as well as the flow of resources, provided by relationships (Greenhaus and Parasuraman, 1994).[16] In the management literature, social support has been primarily addressed in terms of mentoring. Mentoring relationship provide social support in the form of both career development and psychological assistance (Kram, 1985).[17] The most recent conceptualization of mentoring by Higgins and Kram, 2001[18] suggests a developmental network perspective, arguing that individuals may receive assistance from many people at a time. The social support includes the support from work-based and personal sources (Carlson and Perrewe, 1999).[19]

Work-based Social Support

Social support at work may come from the organization at large, immediate supervisors, and co-workers (John *et al.*, 2003).[20] Employees differentiate support from the organization and the support they receive from their immediate work groups or supervisors (Allen, 2001[21]; Self *et al.*, 2005).[22] In the present study, the work-based social supports are classified into support from supervisors and from co-workers.

(i) Support from supervisors

The support given by the supervisors to the workers is in all the work aspects (Goff *et al.*, 1990).[23] The supervisors may provide their support to their subordinates usually or in times of emergency. In the present study, it is measured with the help of the variables drawn from the reviews (Ducharme and Martin, 2000[24]; Kram and Isabella, 1985)[25] and is given in Table 2.2.

Table 2.2: Variables related to the support from supervisors

Sl.No.	Variables
1.	Supervisor is always helping - minded
2.	Supervisor extends his support at the critical time of work
3.	Supervisor understands employees' problem
4.	Supervisor is a participative type
5.	Supervisor provides a flexible schedule to employees
6.	Supervisor is highly generous

(ii) Support from Co-workers

Support from the co-workers provides a moral boost to the employees (Forne, 2003).[26] It represents the helping-minded colleagues and also the supportive behaviour of the co-workers (Rossi, 2001).[27] The peer relationship at work varies from those who exchange information about work and the organization to those who provide confirmation and emotional support (Kirchmeyer, 1992).[28] The support from workers in the present study has been measured with the help of a few variables drawn from the previous studies (Savery, 1988;[29] Buunk and Verhoeven, 1991;[30] Duchame and Martin, 2000).[31] These variables are listed in Table 2.3.

Table 2.3: Variables related to the support from co-workers

Sl.No.	Variables
1.	Co-workers are highly adjustable
2.	Co-workers are highly supportive
3.	Co-workers share responsibilities during emergency
4.	Co-workers are highly informative
5.	Team spirit among the co-workers
6.	Co-workers are taking risks on behalf of me
7.	Co-workers are always sharing their work and life experiences

Personal Social Support

Social support outside work may come from an employee's spouse or partners, parents, children, extended family and friends. Spouse contribute in a variety of areas including earnings and personal financial management (Kate, 1998),[32] home and family responsibility (Bonney *et al.*, 1999),[33] career management and support (Gordon and Whelan-Berry, 2004)[34] and interpersonal support (Becker and Moen, 1999).[35] The personal social support is divided into Domestic and Spouse supports.

(i) Spouse support

It represents the support to an employee by her spouse on financial and non-financial aspects. The variables related to spouse support are drawn from the previous studies (Scadura and Lanker, 1997;[36] and Thomas and Genster, 1995).[37] They are listed in Table 2.4.

Table 2.4: Variables related to spouse support

Sl.No.	Variables
1.	Spouse support in child care activities
2.	Spouse taking care of household chores
3.	Spouse providing financial support
4.	Spouse having a sense of humour
5.	Spouse being supportive to career advancement
6.	Spouse always interacting with me.

(ii) Domestic support

It represents the support of other family members, relatives and friends of the employee. Family, friends, and neighbours may also play significant roles for women who actively juggle the demands of work and home (Bures and Henderson, 1995).[38] Adams *et al.* (1996)[39] found that family-based social support was negatively associated with family interfering with work, which is a dimension of work-family conflict. These relationships also provide supports that reduce work-family conflict by reducing time demands and stress (Seers *et al.*, 1983).[40] The domestic support of employees is measured with the help of the following variables, drawn from the reviews (Parasuraman *et al.*, 1989;[41] 1996;[42] Greenhaus *et al.*, 2003).[43] The variables are given in Table 2.5.

Table 2.5: Variables related to domestic support

Sl.No.	Variables
1.	My family members take care of my children
2.	I have enough support from my family members
3.	Family members help me during financial crisis
4.	Emotional support is given by my relatives and friends
5.	Frequent participation with my family members and friends
6.	I always have my family members who case me

DOMAIN-SPECIFIC DETERMINANTS OF WORK-FAMILY CONFLICT

The work interference with conflict may be caused by some work related variables. Work-specific variables are a source of work-family conflict, because individuals have relatively less control over their work lives than their family lives (Higgins and Duxbury, 1992).[44] There are four role stressors of autonomy, ambiguity, conflict and overload as well as hours spent on paid work.

(i) Role autonomy

According to Hackman (1977),[45] autonomy is the degree at which the job provides substantial freedom, independence and discretion to the individual in scheduling the work and in determining the procedures to be used in carrying it out. Individuals who have control over their work activities have more flexibility in allocating their limited resources at work and at home. As such, the degree of interference from work to family is minimized (Voydanoff, 1988).[46] The degree of role autonomy among the employees has been measured with the help of variables drawn from the previous studies (Pareek and Mehta, 1997;[47] Mathur, 1997).[48] The variables are given in Table 2.6.

Table 2.6: Variables related to role autonomous

Sl.No.	Variables
1.	I have freedom to design my work schedule
2.	I have independence and responsibility in my work
3.	Higher personal responsibility in my work
4.	I create procedures to be used in my work
5.	I have authority to allocate resources
6.	Flexibility in my job is higher

(ii) Role ambiguity

It occurs when an individual does not have clear information about what is expected on the job or how the reward system works (Kahn, *et al.*, 1964). Those who suffer from role ambiguity experience lower levels of job satisfaction, high job-related tension, greater fertility and lower self-confidence (Greenhaus and Bentell, 1985).[49] The role ambiguity among the staff in the present study is measured with the help of six related statement drawn from the previous studies (Srivastav 2006;[50] Pareek, 1983;[51] and Avinash, 2007).[52] The statements are listed in Table 2.7.

Table 2.7: Statements related to role ambiguity

Sl.No.	Variables
1.	Lack of clarity of scope and responsibility on the job
2.	No established procedure in my job
3.	My role in the work is vague
4.	Lack of facts and information given to me about my work
5.	Not knowing the level of expectation of my authorities
6.	My role has been reduced to nothing

(iii) Role conflict

It is the simultaneous occurrence of two or more sets of pressures, such that compliance with one makes compliance with the other more difficult (Kahn *et al.,* 1964). Beehr and McGrath (1992)[53] state that role conflict occurs when an employee is expected, as part of the job, to do something that would conflict with other job or non-job demands or with his or her personal values. Thus, conflict at work may draw resources away from the family conflict (Greenhaus and Bentell, 1985).[54] The role conflict of the employees in the present study has been measured with the help of some statements drawn from the previous studies (Gil-Monke *et al*., 1993[55]; Madhuri and Rachana, 2008;[56] and Tharakan, 1992).[57] The statements are given in Table 2.8.

Table 2.8: Statements related to role conflict

Sl.No.	Variables
1.	I work against my expected role
2.	Incompatible instructions from several people
3.	My values conflict with the organizational values
4.	The expectation of seniors conflict with those of mine
5.	I am unable to satisfy the conflicting demands
6.	I do things acceptable by a few but not all

(iv) Role overload

Role overload occurs when the total demands on time and energy are too great for an individual to perform the role adequately or comfortably (Cooper and Hensman, 1985).[58] Individuals who perceive their workload to be more than they can handle, experience negative emotions, fatigue, tension and other mental health symptoms (Gutek *et al.,* 1991).[59] It is also likely that they will experience higher levels of work interference with family (WIF), because time and energy are limited resources (Grant *et al.,* 1990).[60] The role overload among the employees, in the present study, has been measured with the help of six statements drawn from previous studies (Bernardo, *et al.,* 1987;[61] Lent *et al.,* 1987;[62] Thoits, 1991[63] and Williams *et al.,* 1992).[64] These statements are presented in Table 2.9.

Table 2.9: Statements related to role overload

Sl.No.	Variables
1.	My work load is heavy
2.	I have no sufficient assistance to complete my assignment
3.	I feel over burdened in my role
4.	Too much expectation rests on me
5.	My job assignments are very taxing
6.	Too many suffering hours are imposed on me

WORK TO FAMILY CONFLICT

Work to family conflict occurs, when work demands and responsibilities make it more difficult for an employee to fulfill family role responsibilities (Gogais, 1991).[65] It is a real problem for one, working for larger employers especially in IT industry (Sreekanth, 2007).[66] The work to family conflict has been measured with the help of some related statements by the researchers (Bedeian *et al.,* 1988;[67] Duxlury and Higgins, 1994;[68] Frone *et al.,* 1996;[69] Parasuraman *et al.,* 1996).[70] In the present study, the statements related to the work to family conflict have been drawn from the above said review and presented in Table 2.10.

FAMILY TO WORK CONFLICT

Family to work conflict occurs when family demands and responsibilities make it more difficult for an employee to fulfill work role responsibilities (Adams *et al.,* 1996;[71] Lobel and Clair, 1992).[72]

Table 2.10: Statements related to work-family conflict

Sl.No.	Statements
1.	I feel Physically drained when I get home from work
2.	Due to all pressures at work, when I come home I am too stressed to do the things I enjoy
3.	My work often interferes with my family responsibilities
4.	My work keeps me away from my family activities more than I would like to
5.	The stress from my job often makes me irritable, when I get home
6.	Due to role overload in the work, I am unable to meet my family members
7.	My work affects the amount of time spent with my family members
8.	Due to work pressure, I am unable to share my views with my family members.

The stress at home may be the source of work conflict whereas the sources of family stress are caused by a partner, children, domestic arrangement and environment pressures on the home (Venkatarama Rao, 2005;[73] Lambert, 1990).[74] The performance of a work may be brigtly affected because of the family stress among the employees who is in good working environment (Christen *et al.*, 1990).[75] The family work conflict has been measured by the researchers with relevant statements (Duxlury and Higgin, 1991;[76] Conney and Uhlenbery, 1991;[77] Erickson *et al.*, 2000;[78] Friedman and Greenhaus, 2000;[79] Frone *et al.*, 1992[80] and Frone *et al.*, 1994).[81] The statements used to measure the family to work conflict in the present study are shown in Table 2.11. (*See table on next page*)

ORGANIZATIONAL COMMITMENT

Organizational commitment measures an employee's loyalty to the organization. An individual who has high organizational commitment is willing to exert extra effort on behalf of the organization, and has a strong desire to remain with the organization (Mow day *et al.*, 1979).[82] Organizational commitment refers to an individual's affective reaction to the characters of the employing organization (Cook and Wall, 1980;[83] Decotiis and Summers, 1987).[84]

Table 2.11: Statements related to family to work conflict

Sl.No.	Statements
1.	My family responsibilities prevent me from effectively performing my job
2.	Due to stress at home, I am often preoccupied with family matters at home
3.	The time spent on my family affairs affects the time I have to spend on work
4.	The time spent on my family causes lack of concentration on my work
5.	The strained family relationship leads to stress on work place
6.	Helpless family life creates stress at work place also
7.	Stress caused by the children affects my performance in work
8.	My supervisors and peers dislike my preoccupation with my personal life while at work.

The organizational commitment has been measured by the scale developed by Mow day *et al.,* 1979. The variables related to organizational commitment have been identified with the help of previous research (Baterman and Strasser, 1984;[85] Liou, 1995;[86] Steers, 1997;[87] and Williams and Hazer. 1986).[88] The variables used to measure the organizational commitment among the employees in the present study are shown in Table 2.12.

Table 2.12: Variables related to organizational commitment

Sl.No.	Variables
1.	I would be happy to spend the rest of my career in this organization
2.	I enjoy about discussing the organization with outsiders
3.	I feel as if this organization's problems are my own
4.	I feel as if I am like a part of a family in the organization
5.	I feel emotionally attached to the organization
6.	The organizations mean a lot to me personally
7.	I have a strong sense of belonging to the organization

JOB SATISFACTION

Job satisfaction is the degree at which an individual feels positively or negatively about various aspects of his or her job. Job satisfaction is the result of various attitudes that the worker holds towards his job, towards related factors and towards life in general (Amudha Devi and Velayudhan, 2003).[89] Ibrahim *et al.*, (2004)[90] used 30 items to measure job satisfaction. Job satisfaction was measured through a 28 item "Job Satisfaction Survey Scale" developed by Spector, (1985)[91] consisting of seven dimensions namely pay, promotion, supervision, fringe benefits, operating conditions, co-workers and nature of work. The variables related to job satisfaction have been identified by various researchers (Vaudenberg and Lance, 1992;[92] Currivan, 1999;[93] Blegeu and Muller, 1987;[94] Joshi and Sharma, 1997[95]; Sinha and Singh, 1995[96]; Khan and Robertson, 1992).[97] In the present study, job satisfaction has been measured by the following variables.

Table 2.13: Variables related to job satisfaction

Sl.No.	Variables
1.	Nature of work
2.	Organizational Supervisor
3.	Relationship with co-workers
4.	Pay
5.	Fringe benefits
6.	Scope for promotion or advancement
7.	Job Situation
8.	Work Load
9.	Job Security
10.	Training and Development Opportunities
11.	Sorts of things they do
12.	Ability to meet career goals

JOB STRESS

Job stress is viewed in terms of the incompatibility of work demands. This may be in the form of conflict between organizational demands and one's own values, problems of personal resource allocation, conflict between excessively numerous or difficult tasks. (Duxlury *et al.,* 1995).[98] Working conditions associated with job stress include heavy work loads, role antiquity, under-utilisation of abilities, and lack of participation in decision making, health and safety hazards and job insecurity (Higgins *et al.,* 1993).[99] The job stress variables have been identified with the help of previous researchers (Selye, 1987;[100] Spielberger and Reheliser, 1995[101]; Uma and Kion, 2004).[102] In the present study, the job stress variables have been drawn from various reviews (Arnetz, 1992;[103] Edmundz 2000).[104] These variables are summarized in Table 2.14.

Table 2.14: Variables related to job stress

Sl.No.	Variables
1.	Workload
2.	Complexity of work
3.	Poor leadership
4.	Poor working conditions
5.	Low pay
6.	Monotony of work
7.	Poor career prospects
8.	Work Posture
9.	Discrimination
10.	Low social support
11.	Job insecurity
12.	Too much responsibility
13.	Low participation in decision making
14.	Less liberties
15.	Conflicting demands
16.	Unstandardised pay structure
17.	Absence of human orientation
18.	Flexible labour contract

ABSENTEEISM

Many organization treat absence from work as a measure of hurdles on productivity. While companies expect a certain amount of absenteeism and recognize that some absenteeism is even beneficial to the employee, too much absenteeism can be costly, in terms of productivity and is often symptomatic of problems with the work place (Galinsky *et al.,* 1991).[105] The absenteeism was categorised as:

1. Absenteeism due to ill health,
2. Absenteeism due to family-related problems,
3. Absenteeism due to emotional, physical or mental fatigue and
4. Total absenteeism (total days off due to ill health, child care/ elder care, and physical, mental or emotional exhaustion).

The absenteeism among the employees has been measured with the help of the above mentioned four aspects. The total number days lost by the employees because of their ill health, family-related problems and emotional, physical or mental fatigue have been computed. It is compared with the total working days in the organization. The absenteeism rate has been analysed to exhibit the level of absenteeism among the employees (Ali and Amjadi, 2005).[106]

POSITIVE PARENTING

The National Longitudinal study of children and youth, jointly administered by Statistics, Canada and Human Resources Development, Canada, has identified a number of behaviours which appear to be associated with positive parenting. Five of these behaviours were included in this study. Respondents were asked how often they laughed together with their children, listened to their children's ideas and opinions, ate together as a family, made their children knew they were appreciated, and knew where their children were. Higher scores on this measure reflect greater amount of time spent in behaviours associated with being a good parent. A five point Likert scale was used to collect the responses (1 = never, 2 = monthly, 3 = weekly, 4 = several days per week and 5 = daily). Positive parenting was calculated as the summed average of the five items.

FAMILY INTEGRATION

'Family integration' is defined in terms of the stability of the family unit and the amount of security the family members get, by being part of the family and participating, with the family, in joint activities and functions. An abbreviated five-item version of the Family Integration Scale (FIS), developed by Sebald and Andrews (1962)[107] has been used in this study to measure family integration. A five point likert scale (1 = never, 2 = monthly, 3 = weekly, 4 = several days per week, 5 = daily) was used to collect responses. Family integration was calculated as the summated average of five items (Lowe, 2000[108]; Frone *et al.*, 1997).[109]

PARENTAL SATISFACTION

'Parental satisfaction' is defined to be perceived satisfaction with the parenting role and one's ability as a parent. The three items Kansas Parental Satisfaction Scale developed by Schumm (James *et al.*, 1985)[110] was used in this study to quantity parental satisfaction. The items are drawn from the reviews (Stephens and Tounsend, 1997[111]; Neal *et al.*, 2001;[112] and Stephens *et al.*, 1994).[113] The variables used to measure the parental satisfaction are summarized in Table 2.15.

Table: 2.15: Variables related to parental satisfaction

Sl.No.	Variables
1.	Parenting role
2.	Children's behaviour
3.	Relationship with children
4.	Achievement of the children
5.	Ability to conflict the children
6.	Inter-relationship between the children

FAMILY ADAPTATION

'Family adaptation' is defined as occurring when family members use their strength and capabilities to reduce the demands of the situation, promote individual development of members and achieve a sense of congruency in family functioning (Leske and Jiricka, 1996)[114] Families, high in family adaptation, have a general sense of physical and psychological family health, that is referred to as family well being. The four item Family Adaptation Scale (FAS) developed by Antonovski and Sourani (1988)[115] has been used in this study to measure family adaptation. The variables related to family adaptation among the employees have been identified with the help of previous studies (Lohel, 1991[116]; Rothasen, 1999[117] and Adams *et al.*, 1996).[118] The numbers of variables related to family adaptation are summarized in Table 2.16.

Table 2.16: Variables related to family adaptation

Sl.No.	Variables
1.	Adaptation with the partners
2.	Adaptation with the children
3.	Adaptation with other family members
4.	Adaptation with relatives
5.	Higher family responsibilities
6.	Higher dependent population

FAMILY SATISFACTION

'Family satisfaction' is defined as the degree to which family members feel happy and fulfilled with each other. It includes cohesion, flexibility and communication (Mac Dermind *et al.*, 2000;[119] Voydanoff, 2002).[120] The Kansas Family Life Satisfaction Scale developed by Schumm, Jurich and Bollman (1986)[121] was used to measure family satisfaction in the present study. The variables are listed in Table 2.17.

Table 2.17: Variables related to family satisfaction

Sl.No.	Variables
1.	Degree of closeness with family members
2.	Ability to cope with stress in the family.
3.	Ability to be flexible in the family
4.	Ability to share positive experiences in the family
5.	Quality of communication between family members
6.	Ability to resolve conflicts in the family
7.	Time spent with family members
8.	The way problems are discussed
9.	Fairness of criticism in your family
10.	Family members' concern for each other

The above said ten variables are rated by the employees at five point scale from highly satisfied to high dissatisfied.

LIFE SATISFACTION

Life Satisfaction was operationalized in both the 1991 and 2001 surveys, using Satisfaction With Life Scale (SWLS) (Diener *et al.*, 1985).[122] The SWLS was designed to measure the respondent's global life satisfaction. Higher scores indicate greater levels of life satisfaction. Work-life researchers reason that, because of the interactive and reciprocal nature of the relationships between work and family domains, work-related role stress might combine with work-life demands to exert considerable influence on an employee's overall perception of life satisfaction (Judge *et al.,* 1994).[123] In the present study, the life satisfaction has been measured with the help of five statements (Rice *et al.,* 1980)[124], which are given in Table 2.18.

Table 2.18: Statements related to life satisfaction

Sl.No.	Statements
1.	In most ways my life is close to my ideal.
2.	The conditions of my life are excellent.
3.	I am satisfied with my life.
4.	So far I have got all the important things I want in life.
5.	If I could live my life again, I would change almost nothing.

COPING WITH WORK-FAMILY INTERFACE

'Coping' is defined as the cognitive and behavioural efforts, individuals use to manage taxing demands appraised as exceeding their personal resources (Lazarus and Folkman, 1984).[125] The chronic nature of most contemporary stressors like work-life interface couples individuals to continually cope in order to attenuate the distress. Coping is believed to moderate the effects of stressors on strain (Lazarus, 1991).[126] In the present study, the coping actions adopted by the executives have been identified with the help of previous studies (Havolic and Kennan, 1991;[127] Adams *et al.,* 1996;[128] Jex and Elacqua 1999,[129] and Rontondo *et al.,* 2003).[130] They are listed in Table 2.19.

Table 2.19: Statements in coping strategy

Sl.No.	Statements Related to Coping
1.	I tell myself that time takes care of situations like this
2.	I think that I have done well compared with others in similar situation
3.	I try to work harder and more efficiently
4.	I consult with others to solve my problem
5.	I accept the situation thinking that there is little I can do to change it
6.	I tell myself that I can probably work things out to my advantage
7.	I know myself in my career
8.	I try to avoid the stressful events to a maximum extent
9.	I perceive that this situation will change very soon
10.	I table the problems by myself
11.	I request the help of my boss

References

1. Herman, J.B and Gyllstrom, K.K. (1997), "Working Men and Women: Inter and Intra-role Conflict", *Psychology of Women Quarterly*, 1(1): 319-333.
2. Greenhaus, J.H., Parasuram, S. Ganrose, C.S., Rabinouitz, S and Bentell, N.J. (1989), "Sources of Work-family Conflict among Two-career Couples", *Journal of Vocational Behaviour*, 34(2): 133-153.
3. Bedeian, AG., Burke, B.G., and Moffect, R.G. (1988), "Outcomes of Work-family Conflict among Married Male and Female Professionals", *Journal of Management*, 14(3): 475-491.
4. Pleck, J., Staines, G. and Long, L. (1980), "Conflict between Work and Family Life", *Monthly Labour Review*, 3(1): 29-32.
5. Gutek, B.A., Searle, S. and Klepa, L. (1991), "Gender Role Explanation for Work-family Conflict", *Journal of applied Psychology*, 76(4): 560-568.
6. Wendy, C., Maricuikus, Kareu. S. Whelan – Berry and Judith R. Fordon (2007), "The Relationship of Social Support to the Work-family Balance and Work Outcomes of Middle Women", *Women is Management Review*, 22(2): 86-111.
7. Allen, T., (2001), "Family-supportive Work Environments: The Role of Organizational Perceptions", *Journal of Vocational Behaviour*, 58(6): 414-435.
8. Steffy, B.D., and Jones, J.W. (1998), "The Impact of Family and Career Planning Variables on the Organizational Career, and Community Commitment of Professional Women", *Journal of Vocational Behaviour*, 32(2): 196-212.

9. Lim, V.K.G. and Hian, T.T.S. (1999), "Occupational Stress among Information Technology Personnel in Singapore", www.Occuphealth. fi/e/info/asian/ap 199/Singapore 0.2
10. Kang, Lakhovinder Singh Raghu Bir, (2004), " Identifying Stressors at Work-A Case of Employees in the Electronics Industry", *Decision*, 31(1): 51-72.
11. Howard J.H., (1980), "Stress and Manager: Perspectives", in A.S. Sethi and R.S. Scholer, (Eds), Handbook of Organizational Stress and Coping Strategies, Ballinger, Cambridge, MA.
12. Rajeswari, T.R. (1992), "Employees Stress-A Study with Reference to Bank Employees", *Indian Journal of Industrial Relations*, 27(4): 419-429.
13. Summers, T.P., De Cotiis, T.A., and Ne Nisi, A, S., (1994), "A Field Study of Some Antecedents and Consequences of Job Stress" In P.C. Perreve and R. Cranddl (Eds), Ocuupational Stress: A Handbook, Taylor and Franscis, Washington, DC.
14. Suresh, R.S. and Anantharaman, R.N. (2001), "Job Stress in Police Work", *Indian Journal of Applied Psychology*, 38(1): 17-19.
15. Viswesvaran, C., Sanchaz, J., and Fisher, J. (1999) "The Role of Social Support in the Process of Work Stress: A Meta Analysis", *Journal of Vocational Behaviour*, 54 (1): 314-334.
16. Greenhaus, J., and Parasuraman, S. (1994) "*Work-family Conflict, Social Support and Well-being*", in Dandson, M., and Burke, R., (Eds.) Women in Management: Current Research Issues, Paul Chapman, London, pp. 213-229.
17. Kram, K. (1985), "Men Bring at Work: Developmental Relationships in Organizational Life", Scott, Foresman, Glenview, IL.
18. Higgins, M. and Kram, K. (2001), "Reconceptualizing Men bring at Work: A Developmental Network Perspective", *Academy of Management Review*, 26(2): 284-288.
19. Carlson, D., and Perrewe, P. (1999), "The Role of Social Support in the Stressor-Strain Relationship: An Examination of Work-family Conflict", *Journal of Management*, 25 (4): 513-540.
20. John, E., Thompson, C. and Kopelman, R. (2003), "Rationale and Construct Validity for A Measure of Perceived Organizational Family Support (POFS): Because Purported Practices May Not Reflect Reality", Community, Work and Family, 6 (2): 123-40.
21. Allen, T. (2001), "Family-supportive Work Environments: The Role of Organizational Perceptions", *Journal of Vocational Behaviour*, 58: 414-435.
22. Self, D.R., Holt, D.T. and Schaninger, W.S. (2005), "Work-group and Organizational Support: A Test of Distinct Dimension", *Journal of Occupational and Organizational Psychology*, 78 (1): 133-140.

23. Goff, S., Mount, M. and Janison, R. (1990), "Worker-supervisors' Relationship", International *Journal of Organizational Behaviour*, 11(4): 69-84.

24. Ducharme, L., and Martin, J. (2000), "Unrewarding Work, Co-worker Support, and Job Satisfaction: A Test of the Buffering Hypothesis", *Work and Occupations*, 27 (2): 223-243.

25. Kram, K. and Isabella, L. (1985), "Mentoring Alternatives: The Role of Peer Relationships in Career Development", *Academy of Management Journal*, 28(1): 110-134.

26. Forne, M.R. (2003), "Work-family Balance", in Quick, J.C. and Tetuck, L.E., (Eds.), Handbook of Occupational Health Psychology, *American Psychological Association*, Washington, DC, pp. 143-162.

27. Rossi, A.S. (2001), "Caring and Doing for Others: Social Responsibility in the Domains of Family, Work and Community", University of Chicago Press, Chicago, IL.

28. Kirchmeyer, C. (1992), "Non-work Participation and Work Attitudes: A Test of Scarcity *vs.* Expansion Models of Personal Resources", *Human Relations*, 45: 775-795.

29. Savery, L. (1988), "The Influence of Social Support on the Reaction of An Employee", *Journal of Managerial Psychology*, 3(1): 27-31.

30. Buunk, B. and Verhoeven, K., (1991), "Companionship and Support at Work: A Micro-analysis of the Stress-reducing Features of Social Interaction", *Basic and Applied Social Psychology*, 12 (3): 243-258.

31. Ducharme, L. and Martin, J. (2000), "Unrewarding Work, Co-worker Support and Job Satisfaction: A Test of the Buffering Hypothesis", *Work and Occupations*, 27(2): 223-243.

32. Kate, N. (1998), "Two Careers, One Marriage", American Demographics, 20(4): 2-8.

33. Bonney, J. Kelley, M. and Lerant, R. (1999), "A Model of Father's Behavioural Involvement in Child care in Dual-earner Families", *Journal of Family Psychology*, 13 (3): 401-415.

34. Gordon, J.R. and Whelan-Berry, K.S. (2004), "It Takes Two to Tango: An Empirical Study of Perceived Spousal/Partner Support for Working Women", *Women in Management Review*, 19(5): 260-273.

35. Becker, P. and Moen, P. (1999), "Scaling Back: Dual-earner Couples Work-family Strategies", *Journal of Marriage and the Family*, 61(4): 995-1007.

36. Scadura, T.A., and Lanker, M.J. (1997), "Relationship of Gender, Family Responsibility and Flexible Work Hours to Organizational Commitment and Job Satisfaction", *Journal of Organizational Behaviour*, 18(1): 372-391.

37. Thomas, L.T. and Genster, D.C. (1995), "Impact of Family-supportive Work Variables on Work-family Conflict and Strain-A Control Perspective", *Journal of Applied Psychology*, 80(1): 6-15.

38. Bures, A. and Henderson, D. (1995), "The Effects of Spousal Support and Gender on Worker Stress and Job Satisfaction: A Cross National Investigation of Dual Career Couples", *Journal of Applied Business Research*, 12 (1): 2-9.

39. Adams, A., King, L., and King, D. (1996), "Relationships of Job and Family Involvement, Family Social Support, and Work-family Conflict with Job and Life Satisfaction", *Journal of Applied Psychology*, 81(4): 411-420.

40. Seers, A., Serey, T. and Green, G. (1983), "The Interaction of Job Stress and Social Support: A Strong Inference Investigation", *Academy of Management Journal*, 26(2): 273-284.

41. Parasuraman, S., Greenhaus, J.H., Rabinowitz, S., Bedeian, AG and Moogholder, K.W. (1989), "Work and Family Variables as Mediators of the Relationship between Wives Employment and Husbands' and Well-being", *Academy of Management Journal*, 32(1): 185-201.

42. Parasuraman, S., Purohit, Y.S. and Godshalk, V.M. (1996), "Work and Family Variables, Entrepreneurial Career Success, and Psychological Well-being", *Journal of Vocational Behaviour*, 48: 275-300.

43. Greenhaus, J.H., Collins, K.M. and Shaw, J.D. (2003), "The Relation between Work-family Balance and Quality of Life", *Journal of Vocational Behaviour*, 63(3): 510-531.

44. Higgins, C.A., and Duxbury, L.E. (1992), "Work-family Conflict: A Comparison of Dual Career and Traditional-career Men", *Journal of Organizational Behaviour*, 13(1): 389-411.

45. Hackman, J.R. (1977), "Designing Work for Individuals and for Groups: Perspectives on Behaviour in Organizations", McGraw Hill, New York.

46. Voydanoff, P. (1988), "Work Role Characteristics, Family Structure Demands, and Work-family Conflict", *Journal of Marriage and the Family*, 50 (2): 749-761.

47. Pareek, A. and Mehta, M. (1997), "Role Stress among Working Women" in Pestonjee, D.M. and Pareek, V., (Eds.), Studies in Organizational Role Stress and Copying, Rawat Publications, Jaipur, pp. 173-181.

48. Mathur, S. (1997), "Correlates of Role Stress in Working Women" in Pestorjee, D.M., and Pareek, V., (Eds.), Studies in Organizational Role Stress and Copying, Rawat Publications, Jaipur, pp. 182-190.

49. Greenhaus, J.H. and Bentell, N.J. (1985), "Sources of Conflict between Work and Family Roles", *Academy of Management Review*, 10(1): 76-88.

50. Srivastav, (2006), "Role Stress and Ageing in Organization – An Empirical Study Across Function", *Gitan Journal of Management*, 4(1): 26-39.

51. Pareek, U. (1983), "Organizational Role Stress", in Goodstein, L.D. and J.W. Pfeiffer (Eds.), The 1983 Annual, University Associates, San Diago, California, pp. 115-123.

52. Avinash Kumar Srivastav, (2007), "Stress in Organizational Roles: Individual and Organizational Implications", *The Icfaian Journal of Management Research*, 6(12): 65-74.

53. Beehr, T.A., and Mc Grath, J.E. (1992), "Social Support, Occupational Stress and Anxiety", *Anxiety, Stress and Copying*, 5: 7-19.

54. Greenhaus and Bentell (1985), *Op.cit.*

55. Gil-Monke, P.R., Valcarcel, P., and Zornoza, A. (1993), "Role-stress: Burnout Antecedent in Nursing Professionals", *European Journal of Work and Organizational Psychologist*, 3(3): 217-227.

56. Madhuri Modekurti and Rachana Chattopachyay (2008), "The Relationship between Organizational Role Stress and Life Satisfaction Levels among Women-employees – An Empirical Study", *The Icfai Journal of Management Research*, 7(5): 25-34.

57. Tharakan, P.N. (1992), "Occupational Stress and Job Satisfaction among Working Women", *Journal of the Indian Academy of Applied Psychology*, 18(1 and 2): 37-40.

58. Cooper, C.L. and Hensman, R. (1985), "A Comparative Investigation of Executive Stress: A Ten-nation Study", *Stress Medicine*, 1: 29-38.

59. Gutek, B.A., Searle, S., and Klepa, L. (1991), "Rational *vs.* Gender Role Explanations for Work-family Conflict", *Journal of Applied Psychology*, 76(4): 560-568.

60. Grant, L., Simpson, L.A., and Rong, W.L. (1990), "Gender Parenthood, and Work Hours of Physicians", *Journal of Marriage and the family*, 52(2): 39-49.

61. Bernardo, P.H., Shehar, C.L. and Leslie, G.R. (1987), "A Residue of Tradition; Jobs, Careers and Spouses Time in House Work", *Journal of Marriage and the Family*, 49: 381-390.

62. Lent, R.W., Brown, S.D., and Larkin, K.C. (1987), "Comparison of Three Theoretically Derived Variables in Predicting Career and Academic Behaviour: Self-efficiency, Interest, Congruence, and Consequence Thinking", *Journal of Counselling Psychology*, 34: 293-298.

63. Thoits, P.A. (1991), "On Merging Identity Theory and Stress Research", *Social Psychology Quarterly*, 54: 101-112.

64. Williams, E., Radin, N., and Allegro, T. (1992), "Sex Role Attitudes of Adolescents Reared Primarily by their Fathers: An 11 year follow-up", Merrill-Palmer Quarterly, 38: 457-476.

65. Gogais, B. (1991), "Work-family Conflict: Private Lives – Public Responses", Newyork: Auluun House.

66. Sreekanth, A.K. (2007), "Strategic Employee Attrition Tracking and Analysis", HRD New Gletter, 23(8), November, pp. 28-32.

67. Bedeian, A.G., Burke, B.G. and Proffett, R.G. (1988), "Outcomes of Work-family Conflict among Married Male and Female Professionals", *Journal of Management*, 14(2): 475-49.

68. Duxlury, L and Higgins, C. (1994), "Interference between work and Family: A Comparison by Gender, Family Type, and Perceived Control", *Journal of Family Issues*, 5(1): 449-466.

69. Frone, M.R., Russel, M., and Barnes, G.M. (1996), "Work-family Conflict, Gender, and Health-related Outcomes: A Study of Employed Parents in Low Community Samples", *Journal of Occupational Health Psychology*, 1(1): 57-69.

70. Parasuraman, S., Pruohit, Y.S. Godshalk, V.M., and Bentell, N.J. (1996), "Work and Family Variables, Entrepreneurial Career Success and Psychological well-being", *Journal of Vocational Behaviours*, 48(3): 275-300.

71. Adams, G.A, King, L.A. and King, D.W. (1996), "Relationship of Job and Family Involvement, Family Social Support, and Work-family Conflict with Job and Life Satisfaction", *Journal of Applied Psychology*, 81(14): 411-420.

72. Lobel, S.A. and Clair, L. (1992), "Effects of Family Responsibilities, Gender, and Career Identity Salience on Performance Outcomes", *Academy of Management Journal*, 35(2): 1057-1069.

73. Venkatarama Rao, R. (2005), "The Family Work Conflict among the Employees", The ICFAI *Journal of Organizational Behaviour*, July, pp. 26-44.

74. Lambert, S.J. (1990), "Processes Linking Work and Family: A Critical Review and Research Agender", *Human Relations*, 43(3): 239-257.

75. Christen, K.E. and Staines, G.L. (1990), "Flexi Time: A Viable Solution of Work-family Conflict ?", *Journal of Family Issues*, 11(1): 455-476.

76. Duxlury, L.E. and Higgins, C.A. (1991), "Gender Differences in Work-family Conflict", *Journal of Applied Psychology*, 61(3): 133-146.

77. Conney, T.M. and Uhlenbery, P. (1991), "Changes in Work-family Connections among Highly Educated Men and Women", *Journal of Family Issues*, 12(1): 69-90.

78. Erickson, R.J., Nichols, L. and Ritter, C. (2000), "Family Influence on Absentecism: Testing An Expanded Process Model", *Journal of Vocational Behaviour*, 57 (4): 246-272.

79. Friedman, S.D. and Greenhaus, J.H. (2000), "Work and family – Allies or Enemies? What Happens When Business Professionals Confront Life Choices", New York: Oxford University Press.

80. Frone, M.R., Russel, M. and Cooper, M.C. (1992), "Antecedents and Outcome of Work-family Conflict: Testing a Model of Work-family Interface", *Journal of Applied Psychology*, 73(3): 65-18.

81. Frone, M.R., Russell, M. and Cooper, M.L. (1994), "Relationship between Job and Family Satisfaction: Causal or Non-causal Co Variation", *Journal of Management*, 20(1): 565-579.

82. Mow day, R, Stress, R. and Porter, L. (1979), "The Measurement of Organizational Commitment", *Journal of Vocational Behaviour*, 14(1): 224-227.

83. Cook and Wall, T. (1980), "New Work-attitude Measures of Trust, Organizational Commitment and Personal Need Non-fulfillment", *Journal of Occupational Psychology*, 54(1): 39-52.

84. Decotiis, T.A. and Summers, T.P. (1987), "A Path Analysis of A Model of the Antecedents and Consequences of Organizational Commitment", *Human Relations*, 40(4): 445-470.

85. Baterman, T.S. and Strasser, S. (1984), "A Longitudinal Analysis of the Antecedents of Organizational Commitment", *Academy of Management Journal*, 27(3): 95-112.

86. Liou, K.T. (1995), "Understanding Employee Commitment in the Public Organizations: A Study of the Juvenile Detention Centre", *International Journal of Public Administration*, 18(4): 126-129.

87. Steers, R.M. (1997), "Antecedents and Outcomes of Organizational Commitments", *Administrative Science Quarterly*, 22(2): 46-56.

88. Williams, L.J. and Hazer, J.T. (1986), "Antecedents and Outcomes of Organizational Commitment", *Administrative Science Quarterly*, 22(2): 46-56.

89. Amudha Devi, N.V. and Velayudhan, A. (2003), "Job Satisfaction of Women Lecturers Working in Private and Government Colleges", *Asian Journal of Applied Psychology*, 40: 25-28.

90. Ibrahim, H., Maz-Udulla-Bhat and Al-Medin, A. (2004), "Job Satisfaction and Its Measurement in Private Companies", *Journal of Human Relation Management*, 4(1): 63-76.

91. Spector, M. (1985), Components of Job Satisfaction, *Human Relations*, 16(2): 17-26.

92. Vaudenberg, R.J. and Lance, C.E. (1992), "Examining the Causal Order of Job Satisfaction and Organizational Commitment", *Journal of Management*, 18(3): 153-167.

93. Currivan, D.B. (1999), "The Causal Order of Job Satisfaction and Organizational Commitment in Models of Employee Turnover", *Human Resource Management Review*, 9(1): 495-524.

94. Blegeu, M. and Muller, C.W. (1987), "Nurses Job Satisfaction: A Longitudinal Analysis", *Research in Sociology of Organizations*, 1(1): 75-128.

95. Joshi, R.J. and Baldev R. Sharma, (1997), "Determinants of Managerial Job Satisfaction in a Private Organization", *Indian Journal of Industrial Relations*, 33(10): 48-67.

96. Sinha, J.B.P and Singh, S. (1995), "Employees Satisfaction and Its Organizational Predictors", *Indian Journal of Industrial Relations*, 31(2): 33-45.

97. Khan, H and Robertson, I.T. (1992), "Training and Experience As Predictors of Job Satisfaction and Work Motivation when using Computers: A Correlation of Study", *Behaviour and Information Technology*, 11(1): 53-60.
98. Duxlury, L. and Higgins, (1995), "Obstacles to Productivity: Do you have A Supportive Manager?", Recruitment and Supervision Today, January, 10-11, p. 22.
99. Higgins, C, Duxbury, L. and Lee, C. (1992), "Balancing Work and Family: A Study of the Canadian Private Sector", London, Ontario: National Centre for Research, Management and Development.
100. Selye, H. (1987), "The Stress Concept: Past, Present and Future". In C.L. Cooper (Ed.) "Stress: Myth, Theory and Research", Prentice Hall.
101. Spielberger, C.D. and Reheliser, E.C. (1995), "Measuring Work Stress: The Job Stress Survey", In R. Grandall and P.L. Perrewes(eds)., Occupational Stress: A Hand Work, Washington, DC: Taylors and Francis, pp. 51-69.
102. Uma Bhowon and Ali Kion, J. (2004), "Organizational Climate and Stress: A Study of Managers in Mauritius", *Psychological Studies*, January, pp. 45-51.
103. Arnetz, B., Wiholm, C. (1992), "Technological Stress: Psychological Symptoms in Modern Offices", *Journal of Psychometric Research*, 43(1): 35-42.
104. Edmundz, A., Morris, A. (2000), "The Problem of Information Overload in Business Organization: A Review of Literature", *International Journal of Information Management*, 20(1): 17-28.
105. Galinsky, E., Friedman, D. and Hernandez, C. (1991), "The Corporate Reference Guide to Work-family Programmes", New York, Families and Work Institute.
106. Ali Mollahossgeini and Hossein Amjadi, (2005), "Stress and its Impact on Performance of Staff: A Case Study of Iranian Copper Industry", *Business Respective*, 8(1): 59-69.
107. Seblald, H. and Andrews, H. (1962), "Family Integration and Related Factors in Rural Fringe Population", *Journal of Marriage and Family*, 24(1): 347-351.
108. Lowe, G. (2000), "The Quality of Work – A People Centered Agenda Toronto", Oxford University Press.
109. Frone, M., Russel, M and Cooper, M. (1997), "Relation of Work-family Conflict to Health Outcomes: A Four-year Longitudinal Study of Employed Parents", *Journal of Occupational and Organizational Psychology*, 70(4): 325-335.
110. James, D., Schumm, N., Kennedy, C., Grigshy, C. and Shectman, K. (1985), "Characteristics of Responses to the Kansas Parental Satisfaction Scale among two Samples of Married Parents", *Psychological Reports*, 57(1): 163-169.

111. Stephens, M.A.P and Tounsend, A.C. (1997), "Stress of Parent Care-positive and Negative Effects on Women's Other Roles", *Psychology and Aging*, 12(1): 376-386.

112. Neal, M.B., Dayton, B. and Hammer, L.B. (2001), "Aging Parents Helping Adult Children – The Experience of the Sandwitched Generation", *Family Relations*, 12(1): 314-332.

113. Stephens, M.A., Frants, M.M. and Thousend, A.C. (1994), "Stress and Rewards in Women's Multiple Roles – The Case of Women in the Middle", *Psychology and Aging*, 9(1): 45-52.

114. Leske, J. and Jiricka, M.J. (1996), "Family Concerns: Impact of Family Demands and Family Strengths and Capabilities on Family Well-being and Adaptation after Critical Injury", *American Journal of Critical Care*, 7(5): 187-209.

115. Antonovski, A. and Sourani, T. (1988), "Family Sense of Coherence and Family Adaptation", *Journal of Marriage and the Family*, 50(2): 79-92.

116. Lohel, S.A. (1991), "Allocation of Investment in Work and Family Roles: Alternative Theories and Implication for Research", *Academy of Management Review*, 16(1): 1057-1069.

117. Rothasen, T.J. (1999), "Family in Organizational Research – A Review and Comparison of Definitions and Measures", *Journal of Orgnizational Behaviour*, 20(4): 817-836.

118. Adams, G.A., King, L.A. and King, D.W. (1996), "Relationships of Job and Family Involvement, Family Social Support and Work-family Conflict with Job and use Satisfaction", *Journal of Applied Psychology*, 81(4): 411-420.

119. Mac Dermind, S.M., Barnett, R., Crosby, R., Greenhaus., J., Kobelriz., M.Marks, and S.Perry – Jenkins, (2000), "The Measurement Work-family Satisfaction Relationship", *International Journal of Stress Management*, 36(4): 168-217.

120. Voydanoff, P. (2002), "Linkage between the Work-family Interface and Work-family, and Individual Outcomes: An Integrative Model", *Journal of Family Issue*, 23(1): 138-164.

121. Schumm, W., MC Collum, E., Bugai Ghis, N., Jurich, A. and Bollman, S. (1986), "Characteristics of the Kansas Family Life Satisfaction Scale in a Regional Sample", *Psychological Reports*, 58(6): 975-980.

122. Diener, E., Emmons, R.A., Larsen, R.J., and Griffin, S. (1985), "The Satisfaction with Life Scale", *Journal of Personality Assessment*, 49(4): 71-75.

123. Judge, T.A., Boudreau, J.W and Bretz, R.D., (1994), "Job and Life Attitudes of Male Executives", *Journal of Applied Psychology*, 79(6): 767-782.

124. Rice, R.W., Near, J.P. and Hunt, R.G. (1980), "The Job Satisfaction Life Satisfaction Relationship: A Review of Empirical Research", *Basic and Applied Social Psychology*, 1(1): 37-64.

125. Lazarus, R.S. and Folkman, S. (1984), Stress, Appraisal and coping, Springer, New York.

126. Lazarus, R.S. (1991), "Psychological Stress in the Workplace" *Journal of Social Behaviour and Personality*, 6(7), Handbook on Job Stress, Special Issue, Berreive P.C(Ed), pp. 1-13.

127. Havolic, S.J., and Kennan, J.P.(1991), "Coping with Work Stress: The Influence of Individual Difference", *Journal of Social Behaviour and Personality*, 6(7), Handbook on Job Stress, Special Issue, Penewe, P.C., (Ed.,), pp. 199-212.

128. Adams, G.A., King, L.A., and King, D.W. (1996), "Relationships of Job and Family Involvement, Family Social Support, and Work-family Conflict with Job and Life Satisfaction", *Journal of Applied Psychology*, 81(4): 411-420.

129. Jex, S.M., and Elacqua, T.C. (1999), "Time Management As A Moderator of Relationship between Stressors and Strain", Work and Stress, 13(1): 112-191.

130. Danise M. Rotondo, Dawn, S., Carlson and Joel F. Kin Caid, (2003), "Coping with Multiple Dimensions of Work-family Conflict", *Personnel Review*, 32(3): 275-296.

3 Profile of the Women Employees of Commercial Banks and their Social Support

INTRODUCTION

Work and family domain are mutually influential in both beneficial and deleterious aspects. Characteristics of one's employment, outside the home, have been shown to affect one's functioning at home. Like-wise, the characteristics of one's non-work family life can influence the work life. This spill-over is sometimes inferred by examining the relationship of certain work or family characteristics on the corollary domain, as well as by explicitly asking people about the perceived spill over and/or conflict experienced between family and the work lives.

Explication of the term 'work-family interface' is necessary in order to provide some context. *First*, 'family' is most commonly used in literature as the counterpart to work, although researchers often examine the relationships between work and non-work domains, that encompass other roles than family and to be more inclusive with regard to profile of the employees. The profile of the employees is discussed under three dimensions namely control variables, family domain variables and work domain variables. Since the above said three dimensions are the important causes for the work-family conflict (WFC) and family work conflict (FWC) among the employees, it is included in the present study. Apart from this, in order to provide general information about the women employees, the profile of the employees has been focused upon. The women employees working in public and private sector banks (PSBs and PRBs) have been covered and compared in the present study.

AGE OF THE EMPLOYEES

Age is one the important profiles of the employees which shows their level of maturity and understanding capacity of the individual on work and family problems. Generally, the aged employees have more work-life balance than the youngsters because of their experience in their life. In the present study, the age of the employees is confined to less than 25 years, 25 to 30, 31 to 35, 36 to 40, 41 to 45 and above 45 years. The distribution of employees on the basis of their age is given in Table 3.1.

Table 3.1: Age of the employees

Sl.No.	Age (in years)	Number of Employees in		Total
		PSBs	PRBs	
1.	Less than 25	25(8.06)	16(14.41)	41(9.74)
2.	25 – 30	32(10.32)	34(30.63)	66(15.68)
3.	31 – 35	71(22.91)	36(32.43)	107(25.42)
4.	36 – 40	89(28.71)	11(9.91)	100(23.75)
5.	41 – 45	61(19.68)	8(7.21)	69(16.38)
6.	Above 45	32(10.32)	6(5.41)	38(9.03)
	Total	**310(100)**	**111(100)**	**421(100)**

Note: Figures in brackets indicate percentage

Table 3.1 shows that the important age group among the employees are 31 to 35 years and 36 to 40 years which constitute 25.42 and 23.75 per cent of the total respectively. The number of employees in the age category of above 45 years constitute 9.03 per cent of the total. The important age group among the employees in PSBs is 36 to 40 years and 31 to 35 years constituting 28.71 and 22.90 per cent of their total respectively. Among the employees in PRBs, these two are 31 to 35 and 25 to 30 years which constitute 32.43 and 30.63 per cent to their total respectively. The analysis reveals that the age of the employees in PRBs is comparatively less than the employees in the PSBs.

EDUCATIONAL QUALIFICATION AMONG THE EMPLOYEES

The level of education may have its own influence on the work-family interact among the employees. The level of education provides more knowledge and level of tolerance and understanding of the work, family life and also the work life balance. Hence, it is included as one of the profile variables of the present study. The educational qualification among the employees is confined to engineering, MCA, MBA, post graduation and under-graduation. The distribution of employees on the basis of their level of education is shown in Table 3.2.

Table 3.2: Educational qualification of the employees

Sl.No.	Educational Qualification	Number of Employees in		Total
		PSBs	PRBs	
1.	Engineering	29 (9.35)	9(8.11)	38(9.03)
2.	MCA	22(7.10)	8(7.21)	30(7.12)
3.	MBA	41(13.23)	16(14.41)	57(13.54)
4.	Post-graduation	79(25.48)	36(32.43)	115(27.32)
5.	Under-graduation	139(44.84)	42(37.84)	181(42.99)
	Total	**310(100)**	**111(100)**	**421(100)**

Note: Figures in brackets indicate percentage

Table 3.2 reveals that the important levels of education among the employees are under graduation and post graduation since they constitute 42.99 and 27.32 per cent of the respective total. The most important educational qualifications among the employees in PSBs are under graduation and post graduation which constitute 44.84 and 25.48 per cent to their totals respectively. Among the employees in PRBs, these two are under-graduation and post-graduation which constitute 37.84 and 32.43 per cent of their respective total. The analysis reveals that majority of the employees in PSBs and PRBs are having the educational qualification of under graduation, and post-graduation.

PERSONAL INCOME OF THE EMPLOYEES

'Personal income' represents the income earned by an employee from her bank during the period of one month. Since the personal income provides a monetary pack up of the employees, and it may have influence on the perception on her work and family, it is included as one of the profiles of the employees. Sometimes, higher personal income may solve the work-family conflict and family-work conflict.

In the present study, the monthly personal income of the employees is confined to less than Rs. 15,000, Rs. 15,000 to 25,000; Rs. 25,001 to 35,000; Rs. 35,001 to 45,000 and above Rs. 45,000. The personal income of the employees is given in Table 3.3.

Table 3.3: Distribution of employees based on the personal income per month

Sl.No.	Personal Income per Month	Number of Employees in		Total
		PSBs	PRBs	
1.	Less than Rs. 15,000	18(5.81)	21(18.92)	39(9.27)
2.	Rs. 15,000 - 25,000	46(14.84)	33(29.73)	79(18.77)
3.	Rs. 25,001 - 35,000	93(30)	31(27.93)	124(29.45)
4.	Rs. 35,001 - 45,000	98(31.61)	18(16.22)	116(27.55)
5.	Above Rs. 45,000	55(17.74)	8(7.20)	63(14.96)
	Total	**310(100)**	**111(100)**	**421(100)**

Note: Figures in brackets indicate percentage

The important categories of personal income per month among the employees are Rs. 25,001 to 35,000 and Rs. 35,001 to 45,000 which constitute 29.45 and 27.55 per cent of their respective total. The number of employees earning a monthly income of above Rs. 45,000 constitutes 14.96 per cent of the total. The most important categories of personal income per month, among the employees in PSBs are Rs. 35,001 to 45,000 and Rs. 25,001 to 35,000 which constitute 31.61 and 30.00 per cent of their respective total. Among the employees in PRBs, the important income categories are Rs. 15,000 to 25,000 and Rs. 25,001 to 35,000 which constitute 29.73 and 27.93 per cent of their respective total. The analysis reveals that the monthly personal income among the employees in PSBs is identified as greater compared to the monthly income of the employees in PRBs.

YEARS OF EXPERIENCE OF THE EMPLOYEES

The 'years of experience' indicate the number of years the employees have worked in the related field. Since, the years of experience may have effect on the level of tolerance and the balance in work and life of the employees, it is included as one of the profile variables. The experienced employees may have less work-life imbalance compared to the lesser experienced employees. The years of experience among the employees in the present study is confined to less than 3 years, 3 to 6 years, 6 to 9 years, 9 to 12 years and above 12 years. The distribution of employees on the basis of their years of experience is given in Table 3.4.

Table 3.4: Distribution of the employees based on their years of experience

Sl.No.	Years of Experience	Number of Employees in		Total
		PSBs	PRBs	
1.	Less than 3 years	32(10.32)	7(6.31)	39(9.27)
2.	3 - 6 years	69(22.26)	12(10.81)	81(19.24)
3.	6 - 9 years	73(23.55)	19(17.12)	92(21.85)
4.	9 - 12 years	88(28.39)	37(33.33)	125(29.69)
5.	Above 12 years	48(15.48)	36(32.43)	84(19.95)
	Total	**310(100)**	**111(100)**	**421(100)**

Note: Figures in brackets indicate percentage

The important numbers of years of experience among the employees are 9 to 12 years and 6 to 9 years which constitute 29.69 and 21.85 per cent of their respective total. The number of employees with an experience of above 12 years constitutes 19.95 of the total. The most important years of experience among the employees in PSBs are 9 to 12 years and 6 to 9 years which constitute 28.39 and 23.55 per cent of their respective total. The most important years of experiences among the employees in PRBs are 9 to 12 years and above 12 years which constitute 33.33 and 32.43 per cent of their respective total. The analysis infers that the years of experience among the employees in PRBs is greater than the level of experience among the employees in PSBs.

MARITAL STATUS OF THE EMPLOYEES

One of important family domain variables among the employees is their marital status. Since, the marital status may have its own influence on their family responsibilities and also family-work conflict, it is included as one of the family domain variables. In the present study, the marital status among the employees is confined to unmarried, married, divorced and widow. The distribution of employees on the basis of their marital status is presented in Table 3.5.

Table 3.5: Marital status of the employees

Sl.No.	Marital Status	Number of Employees in		Total
		PSBs	PRBs	
1.	Unmarried	22(7.10)	14(12.61)	36(8.55)
2.	Married	266(85.81)	88(79.28)	354(84.09)
3.	Divorced	18(5.80)	8(7.21)	26(6.18)
4.	Widow	4(1.29)	1(0.90)	5(1.18)
	Total	**310(100)**	**111(100)**	**421(100)**

Note: Figures in brackets indicate percentage

The important marital status among the employees are 'married' and 'unmarried' which constitute 84.09 and 8.55 per cent of their respective total. The most important marital status among the employees in PSBs is 'married' which constitutes 85.81 per cent of its total whereas among the employees in PRBs also, it is 'married' but constitutes 79.28 per cent of its total. The analysis reveals that the most important marital status among the employees is 'married'.

TYPE OF FAMILY OF THE EMPLOYEES

The type of family indicates nuclear or joint family system followed by the employees. Since the type of family may be related with the level of importance attached with work and family, work-family conflict and family-work conflict, it is included as one of the profile variables. The distribution of employees on the basis of the type of the family is presented in Table 3.6.

Table 3.6: Distribution of employees based on the type of family

Sl.No.	Type of Family	Number of Employees in		Total
		PSBs	PRBs	
1.	Nuclear	281(90.65)	102(91.89)	383(90.97)
2.	Joint	29(9.35)	9(8.11)	38(9.03)
	Total	**310(100)**	**111(100)**	**421(100)**

Note: Figures in brackets indicate percentage

A maximum of 90.97 per cent of the employees are following nuclear family system as seen from the above Table 3.6. The most important type of family among the employees in PSBs is 'nuclear family system' which constitutes 90.65 per cent of its total. Among the employees in PRBS, it is also 'nuclear family system' which constitutes 91.89 per cent of its total. The analysis reveals that the important family system among the employees is 'nuclear family system'.

FAMILY SIZE OF THE EMPLOYEES

The family size represents the number of family members living along with the employees. Since the family size has its own influence on the family-work conflict and work-life imbalance among the employees, it is included as one of the profile variables. The family size of the employees is confined to less than 3 members, 3 to 4 members, 5 to 6 members, 7 to 8 members and above 8 members. The distribution of employees on the basis of their family size is given in Table 3.7.

Table 3.7: Distribution of the employees based on the family size

Sl.No.	Family Size	Number of Employees in		Total
		PSBs	PRBs	
1.	Less than 3 members	27(8.71)	12(10.81)	39(9.26)
2.	3 - 4 members	218(70.32)	58(52.25)	276(65.56)
3.	5 - 6 members	49(15.81)	28(25.23)	77(18.29)
4.	7 - 8 members	12(3.87)	10(9.01)	22(5.23)
5.	Above 8 members	4(1.29)	3(2.70)	7(1.66)
	Total	**310(100)**	**111(100)**	**421(100)**

Note: Figures in brackets indicate percentage

The important family sizes of the employees are 3 to 4 members and 5 to 6 members which constitute 65.56 and 18.29 per cent of their respective total. The number of employees with the family size of above 8 members, constitutes 1.66 per cent of the total. The most important family size of the employees in PSBs are 3 to 4 members and 5 to 6 members which constitute 70.32 and 15.81 per cent of their respective total. Among the employees in PRBs, these are also 3 to 4 members and 5 to 6 members which constitute 52.25 and 25.23 per cent of their respective total. The analysis reveals that the most important family size among the employees in PSBs and PRBs is 3 to 4 members.

NUMBER OF EARNING MEMBERS PER FAMILY AMONG THE EMPLOYEES

Since the number of earning members in the family is highly associated with the work-life imbalance and work-family interface, it is included as one of the profile variables in the present study. The number of earning members in the present study is confined to one, two, three and more than three. The distribution of employees on the basis of the number of earning members per family is given in Table 3.8.

Table 3.8: Number of earning members per family

Sl.No.	Number of Earning Members	Number of Employees in		Total
		PSBs	PRBs	
1.	One	47(15.16)	13(11.71)	60(14.25)
2.	Two	232(74.84)	76(68.47)	308(73.16)
3.	Three	19(6.13)	14(12.61)	33(7.84)
4.	More than three	12(3.87)	8(7.21)	20(4.75)
	Total	**310(100)**	**111(100)**	**421(100)**

Note: Figures in brackets indicate percentage

From Table 3.8 it is seen that, a maximum of 73.16 per cent of the employees have two earning members in their family. This is followed by only one earning member which constitutes 14.25 per cent of the total. The most important number of earning members among the employees in PSBs is two which constitutes 74.84 per cent of the total whereas among the employees in PRBs, it is also two earning members constituting 68.47 per cent of its total. The analysis infers that the important number of earning members per family among the employees is two.

LEVEL OF EDUCATION OF THE SPOUSE OF THE EMPLOYEES

The level of education of the spouse may enrich the level of understanding and adjustment in life, whereas sometimes, it may be one of the causes for work-life imbalance also. Since, the level of education of the spouse is associated with the work-life imbalance, it has been included in the present study as one of the profile variables. The level of education of the spouse is confined to Engineering,

MBA, MCA, Post-graduation, Under-graduation and others. The distribution of employees on the basis of the level of education of their spouse is given in Table 3.9.

Table 3.9: Distribution of the employees based on the level of education of spouse

Sl.No.	Level of Education of Spouse	Number of Employees in		Total
		PSBs	PRBs	
1.	Engineering	81(30.45)	22(25)	103(29.10)
2.	MBA	24(9.02)	13(14.77)	37(10.45)
3.	MCA	19(7.15)	18(20.45)	37(10.45)
4.	Post-graduation	85(31.95)	26(29.55)	111(31.36)
5.	Under-graduation and others	57(21.43)	9(10.23)	66(18.64)
	Total	**266(100)**	**88(100)**	**354(100)**

Note: Figures in brackets indicate percentage

The important level of education of the spouse is post graduation which alone constitutes 31.36 per cent of the total married employees. It is followed by engineering graduates which constitute 29.10 per cent of the total. The most important levels of education of the spouse of the employees in PSBs are post graduation and engineering which constitute 31.95 and 30.45 per cent of their respective totals. In the case of PRBs, the levels of education of the spouse of employees are also post-graduation and engineering which constitute 29.55 and 25.00 per cent of their respective total. The analysis infers that the important levels of education of the spouse of the employees are post graduation and engineering.

EMPLOYMENT OF SPOUSE

The employment of the spouse may influence different dimensions in their work-family interface. The nature of understanding in their work-life interface may be different among different employees since the nature of employment plays an important role in the determination of work-family conflict. Hence the 'nature of employment of spouse' is also included as one of the profile variables. The employment of spouse is shown in Table 3.10.

Table 3.10: Distribution of employees based on the employment of spouse

Sl.No.	Employment of Spouse	Number of Employees in		Total
		PSBs	PRBs	
1.	Employed	254(95.49)	83(94.32)	337(95.19)
2.	Unemployed	12(4.51)	5(5.68)	17(4.81)
	Total	**266(100)**	**88(100)**	**354(100)**

Note: Figures in brackets indicate percentage

The above Table 3.10 reveals that, a maximum of 95.19 per cent of the employees have their spouses employed whereas only 4.81 per cent of the employees have unemployed spouses. Among the employees in PSBs, the number of employees having employed spouse constitutes 95.49 per cent of its total whereas among the employees in PRBs, it constitutes 94.32 per cent of its total. The analysis reveals that most of employees' spouses are employed.

PARENTAL STATUS OF THE EMPLOYEES

The parental status indicates the status of the employees in their family life and reveals if they are just married or married or with kids. Since the parental status of the employees has its own influence on their family role and responsibilities, it may be one of the causes of work family interface. Hence, it is included as one of the profile variables. The parental status of the employees in the present study is classified into 'with children' and 'without children'. The distribution of employees on the basis of their parental status is given in Table 3.11.

Table 3.11: Distribution of the employees based on parental status

Sl.No.	Parental Status	Number of Employees in		Total
		PSBs	PRBs	
1.	With Children	267(92.71)	85(87.63)	352(91.43)
2.	Without Children	21(7.29)	12(12.37)	33(8.57)
	Total	**288(100)**	**97(100)**	**385(100)**

Note: Figures in brackets indicate percentage

The above Table 3.11 reveals that, a maximum of 91.43 per cent of the employees are having children whereas only 8.57 per cent of the employees are not having any child. Among the employees in PSBs, the number of employees with children alone constitutes 92.71 per cent of the total. Among the employees in PRBs, it constitutes 87.63 per cent of the total. The analysis infers that most of the married employees are having children.

AGE OF THE YOUNGEST CHILD

One of the important family domain variables is the age of the youngest child. Since the age of the youngest child may influence the degree of child care in their family, it is included as one of the profile variables. The lesser age of the youngest child requires more child care than the other children. It may lead to some work-life imbalance. The age of the youngest child in the present study is confined to less than 2 years, 2 to 4 years, 4 to 6 years, 6 to 8 years and above 8 years. The distribution of employees on the basis of the age of their youngest child is presented in Table 3.12.

Table 3.12: Distribution of the employees on the basis of the age of the youngest child

Sl.No.	Age of the Youngest Child	Number of Employees in		Total
		PSBs	PRBs	
1.	Less than 2 years	61(22.85)	17(20)	78(22.16)
2.	2 - 4 years	84(31.46)	26(30.59)	110(31.25)
3.	4 - 6 years	51(19.10)	22(25.88)	73(20.74)
4.	6 - 8 years	46(17.23)	9(10.59)	55(15.62)
5.	Above 8 years	25(9.36)	11(12.94)	36(10.23)
	Total	**267(100)**	**85(100)**	**352(100)**

Note: Figures in brackets indicate percentage

The important age groups of the youngest child of the employees are 2 to 4 years and less than 2 years which constitute 31.25 and 22.16 per cent of the respective total. The number of employees with the youngest child with the age of above 8 years constitutes 10.23 per cent of the total. The most important age group of the youngest child of the employees in PSBs is 2 to 4 years which constitutes 31.46 per cent of the total. Among the employees in PRBs, it is also 2 to 4 years constituting 30.59 per cent of the total. The analysis reveals that youngest child of most of the employees belong to the age of 2 to 4 years.

MONTHLY FAMILY INCOME OF THE EMPLOYEES

The family income represents the total income earned by all family members of the employees during the period of one month. Since the family income of the employees, has its own influence on the financial position of the family, it is included as one of the profile variables. In general, the employees with higher family income may make so many arrangements to get their family work done. It may relax them from their family responsibilities. Sometimes, higher family income is one of the causes for the work-life imbalance. The family income of the employees is shown in Table 3.13.

Table 3.13: Family income per month of the employees

Sl.No.	Family Income per Month	Number of Employees in		Total
		PSBs	PRBs	
1.	Less than Rs. 25,000	16(5.16)	15(13.51)	31(7.36)
2.	Rs. 25,000 - 35,000	33(10.64)	21(18.92)	54(12.83)
3.	Rs. 35,001 - 45,000	129(41.61)	38(34.23)	167(39.67)
4.	Rs. 45,001 - 55,000	68(21.94)	24(21.62)	92(21.85)
5.	Above Rs. 55,000	64(20.65)	13(11.72)	77(18.29)
	Total	**310(100)**	**111(100)**	**421(100)**

Note: Figures in brackets indicate percentage

The above Table 3.13 reveals that the important family income groups of the employees are Rs. 35,001 to 45,000 and Rs. 45,001 to 55,000 which constitute 39.67 and 21.85 per cent of their respective totals. The employees with the family income of above Rs. 55,000 per month constitute 18.29 of the total. The important level of family income groups among the employees in PSBs are Rs. 35,001 to 45,000 and Rs. 45,001 to 55,000 which constitutes 41.61 and 21.94 per cent of their respective totals. Among the employees in PRBs, the important income groups are Rs. 35,001 to 45,000 and Rs. 45,001 to 55,000 which constitute 34.23 and 21.62 per cent of their respective totals. The analysis reveals that the family income of the employees in the PSBs is greater than the income of the employees in the PRBs.

CARE RESPONSIBILITIES AMONG THE EMPLOYEES

Care responsibilities indicate the responsibilities of the employees in taking care of their children and adults who depend on them. Since the caring responsibilities have their own influence on the family responsibilities and ultimately on the work family interface, it is included as one of the profile variables in the present study. The caring responsibilities of the employees are listed with the help of six responsibilities. The employees are asked to rate these six responsibilities at five point scale from very high to very low. The assigned marks on these scales are from 5 to 1 respectively. The mean score of the caring responsibilities among the employees have been computed and presented in Table 3.14.

Table 3.14: Mean score of caring responsibilities among the employees

Sl. No.	Family Responsibilities	Mean Score among the Employees in		't' statistic
		PSBs	PRBs	
1.	Child Care	3.2445	3.9452	-2.2417*
2.	Elder Care	3.0245	2.4517	1.3816
3.	Caring sick child	3.1504	3.8673	-2.1085*
4.	Caring disabled child	3.2083	3.9152	-2.4508*
5.	Caring sick adults	3.1144	2.9945	0.3317
6.	Caring disabled adult	3.1506	3.0308	0.2302
	Overall	3.1321	3.3675	-0.6048

* *Significant at five per cent level.*

From Table 3.14, it is seen that among the employees in PSBs, the caring responsibilities with highest mean scores have been noticed in the case of 'child care' and 'caring disabled child' since their respective mean scores are 3.2445 and 3.2083. Among the employees in PRBs, the high scoring caring responsibilities are 'child care' and 'caring disabled child' since their mean scores are 3.9452 and 3.9152 respectively. Regarding the caring responsibilities, the significant difference among the employees in PSBs and PRBs has been noticed in the case of 'child care', 'caring sick child' and 'disabled child' since their respective 't' statistics are significant at five per cent level. Regarding the overall caring responsibilities, there is no significant difference noticed among the employees in PSBs and PRBs.

TIME DEVOTED TO FAMILY WORK AMONG EMPLOYEES

The time devoted to family work is one of the important causes for work family interface, and therefore it is included as one of the profile variables. More time devoted to family works creates problem in their work whereas less time devoted may lead to problem in the family. There should be a balance between both the works and in the present study the time is confined to less than 1 hour, 1 to 2 hours, 2 to 3 hours, 3 to 4 hours and above 4 hours per day. The distribution of employees on the basis of their time devoted to their family is given in Table 3.15.

Table 3.15: Distribution of employees based on the time devoted to family work per day

Sl. No.	Time Devoted to Family Work per Day	Number of Employees in		Total
		PSBs	PRBs	
1.	Less than 1 hour	61(19.68)	13(11.71)	74(17.58)
2.	1 - 2 hours	96(30.97)	17(15.32)	113(26.84)
3.	2 - 3 hours	72(23.23)	35(31.53)	107(25.42)
4.	3 - 4 hours	49(15.80)	27(24.32)	76(18.05)
5.	Above 4 hours	32(10.32)	19(17.12)	51(12.11)
	Total	**310(100)**	**111(100)**	**421(100)**

Note: Figures in brackets indicate percentage

The above Table 3.15 reveals that the important time categories devoted to family work per day among the employees are 1 to 2 hours and 2 to 3 hours, which constitute 26.84 and 25.42 per cent of their respective totals. The employees who spend above 4 hours for family work per day constitute 12.11 per cent of the total respondents. The important time categories devoted to family per day among the employees in PSBs are 1 to 2 hours and 2 to 3 hours which constitute 30.97 and 23.23 per cent of their respective totals. Among the employees in PRBs, these are 2 to 3 hours and 3 to 4 hours constituting by 31.53 and 24.32 per cent of the employees in PRBs respectively.

The analysis reveals that the time devoted to family work is identified as higher among the employees in PRBs than that among the employees in PRBs.

DESIGNATION IN THE ORGANIZATION

The designation among the employees may have its own influence on the work life balance and also work family interface. Hence it is included as one of the profile variables. The designation of the employees in the present study is confined to higher and middle level management. The distribution of employees on the basis of their designation is shown in Table 3.16.

Table 3.16: Distribution of employees based on their designation in the organization

Sl. No.	Designation	Number of Employees in		Total
		PSBs	PRBs	
1.	Higher level management (Manager and Assistant Managers)	62(20)	19(17.12)	81(19.24)
2.	Middle level management (Staff) (Clerks and cashiers)	248(80)	92(82.88)	340(80.76)
	Total	**310(100)**	**111(100)**	**421(100)**

Note: Figures in brackets indicate percentage

From the above Table 3.16 it could be seen that the important designation among the employees in the present study is middle level management which constitutes 80.76 per cent of the total respondents. It is followed by the designation of higher level management which constitutes 19.24 per cent of the total. The most important designation among the employees in PSBs is middle level management which constitutes 80.00 per cent of the total employees. Among the employees in PRBs, it is also middle level management which constitutes 82.88 per cent of the total respondents. The analysis reveals that majority of the employees belong to middle level management.

HOURS WORKED PER DAY BY THE EMPLOYEES

The total number of hours worked per day by the employees may have its influence on the work family interface. The higher quantum of work load and number of working hours may have their own influence on the work-family interface, and so it has been included as one of the profile variables. The hours worked per day by the employees in the present study is confined to less than 8 hours, 8 to 9 hours, 9 to 10 hours, 10 to 11 hours and above 11 hours. The distribution of employees on the basis of the hours they worked per day is given in Table 3.17.

Table 3.17: Distribution of employees based on the hours worked per day

Sl.No.	Hours Worked per Day	Number of Employees in		Total
		PSBs	PRBs	
1.	Less than 8 hours	18(5.81)	–	18(4.28)
2.	8 to 9 hours	102(32.90)	6(5.40)	108(25.65)
3.	9 to 10 hours	93(30)	28(25.23)	121(28.74)
4.	10 to 11 hours	71(22.90)	33(29.73)	104(24.70)
5.	Above 11 hours	26(8.39)	44(39.64)	70(16.63)
	Total	**310(100)**	**111(100)**	**421(100)**

Note: Figures in brackets indicate percentage

The above Table 3.17 reveals that a maximum of 28.74 per cent of the employees work 9 to 10 hours per day which is followed by 8 to 9 hours per day by 25.65 per cent of the total employees. The most important hours of duty per day among the employees in PSBs are 8 to 9 hours and 9 to 10 hours which constitute by 32.90 and 30.00 per cent of their respective totals. Among the employees in PRBs, these are above 11 hours and 10 to 11 hours per day which constitute 39.64 and 29.73 per cent of their respective totals. The analysis reveals that the hours worked per day by the employees in PRBS is greater than the hours worked per day by the employees in PSBs.

WORKING SCHEDULE OF THE EMPLOYEES

The working schedule indicates the regularity of the working hours prescribed by the organization. Since the working schedule may influence on the work-family interface, it is included as one of the profile variables. The working schedule among the employees in the present study is classified into regular, partially regular and irregular. The distribution of employees on the basis of their working schedule is given in Table 3.18.

Table 3.18: Distribution of employees based on the working schedule

Sl.No.	Working Schedule	Number of Employees in		Total
		PSBs	PRBS	
1.	Regular	183(59.03)	32(28.83)	215(51.07)
2.	Partially regular	102(32.90)	43(38.74)	145(34.44)
3.	Irregular	25(8.07)	36(32.43)	61(14.49)
	Total	**310(100)**	**111(100)**	**421(100)**

Note: Figures in brackets indicate percentage

From Table 3.18, it is seen that a maximum of 51.07 per cent of the employees are having regular working schedule which is followed by partially regular working schedule constituting 34.44 per cent of the total employees. The important working schedules among the employees in PSBs are regular and partially regular which constitute 59.03 and 32.90 per cent of their respective totals whereas for the employees in PRBs these schedules are partially regular and irregular which constitute 38.74 and 32.43 per cent of their respective totals. The analysis reveals that the employees in PRBs have a higher irregular working schedule than the employees in the PSBs.

SOCIAL SUPPORT OF THE EMPLOYEES

The social supports of the employees are classified into personal social support and work-based support. The personal-social support is again classified into spouse-support and domestic-support. The spouse support of the employees has been measured with the help of six variables which are measured at five point scale. The mean scores of variables in spouse-support among the employees in PSBs and PRBs have been computed separately to exhibit the level of spouse-support among the employees. Regarding the variables in spouse support, the significant difference among the employees in PSBs and PRBs have been examined with the help of 't' test. The results are given in Table 3.19. (*See table on next page*)

The highly perceived variables among the employees in PSBs are spouse always interacting with me and 'spouse providing financial support' since their mean scores are 3.9432 and 3.9188 respectively. Among the employees in PRBs, these two are 'spouse having a sense of humour' and 'spouse is supportive' to my career development" since their mean scores are 3.7088 and 3.1146 respectively.

Table 3.19: Spouse Support (SS) among the employees

Sl. No.	Variables in SS	Mean Score among the Employees in		't' statistics
		PSBs	PRBs	
1.	Spouse support in child-care activities	3.4143	2.6526	2.3486*
2.	Spouse taking care of household chores	3.6033	2.8144	2.6093*
3.	Spouse providing financial support	3.9188	3.0245	2.7034*
4.	Spouse having a sense of humour	3.6244	3.7088	-0.2642
5.	Spouse being supportive to my career development,	3.5028	3.1146	1.0149
6.	Spouse always interacting with me	3.9432	3.0424	2.7081*

* *Significant at five per cent level.*

Regarding the perception on variables related to spouse support, the significant difference among the two groups of employees has been noticed in the case of four variables in spouse support out of 6 variables, which are higher among the employees in PSBs than among employees in PRBs.

Score on Spouse Support (SSS) among the Employees

The scores of the variables in spouse support among the employees have been included for the reliability analysis. The reliability co-efficient (0.7438) indicates that the included six variables in spouse support explain it to an extent of 74.38 per cent. The Score on Spouse Support (SSS) among the employees has been computed by the mean score of the variables in it. The SSS in the present study is confined to less than 2.00; 2.00-3.00; 3.01-4.00 and above 4.00. The distribution of employees on the basis of their SSS is presented in Table 3.20.

Table 3.20 reveals that the important SSS among the employees are 3.01 to 4.00 and 2.00 to 3.00 which constitute 34.44 and 30.40 per cent of their respective total. The employees with the SSS of above 4.00 constitute 15.68 per cent of the total employees.

Table 3.20: Distribution of employees based on the score on spouse support (SSS)

Sl.No.	SSS	Number of Employees in		Total
		PSBs	PRBs	
1.	Less than 2.00	68(21.94)	14(12.61)	82(19.48)
2.	2.00 - 3.00	86(27.74)	42(37.84)	128(30.40)
3.	3.01 - 4.00	109(35.16)	36(32.43)	145(34.44)
4.	Above 4.00	47(15.16)	19(17.12)	66(15.68)
	Total	**310(100)**	**111(100)**	**421(100)**
Reliability co-efficient: 0.7438				

Note: Figures in brackets indicate percentage

The important SSS among the employees in PSBs are 3.01 to 4.00 and 2.00 to 3.00 which constitute 35.16 and 27.74 per cent of their respective totals. Among the employees in PRBs, these two SSS are 2.00 to 3.00 and 3.01 to 4.00 which constitute 37.84 and 32.43 per cent of their respective totals. The analysis reveals that the spouse support among the employees in PSBs is greater than that among the employees in PRBs.

DOMESTIC SUPPORT AMONG THE EMPLOYEES

It represents the support of family members, relatives and friends of the employees. In the present study, the domestic support to the employees has been measured with the help of six variables drawn from the reviews. The variables are measured at five point scale. The mean scores of the six variables among the employees in PSBs and PRBs have been computed separately, to show the domestic support among the two groups of bank employees. The 't' test has been used to find out the significant difference between the two groups of employees regarding their view on domestic support. The results are shown in Table 3.21. (*See table on next page*)

The highly viewed domestic support variables among the employees in PSBs are 'I always have my family members who care for me' and 'frequent participation with my family members and friends' since their mean scores are 3.8028 and 3.7314 respectively.

Table 3.21: Domestic support among the employees (DS)

Sl. No.	Variables	Mean Score among the Employees in		't' statistics
		PSBs	PRBs	
1.	My family members take care of my children	3.6024	2.8144	2.4544*
2.	I have enough support from my family members	2.9908	2.5146	1.6509
3.	Family members help me during financial crisis	3.4142	2.8042	2.0617*
4.	Emotional support is given by my relatives and friends	2.9091	3.2145	-0.5163
5.	Frequent participation with my family members and friends	3.7341	2.6608	2.8617*
6.	I always have my family members who care for me	3.8028	3.0819	2.5085*

** Significant at five per cent level.*

Among the employees in PRBs, these two are 'emotional support is given by my relatives and friends' and 'I always have my family members who care for me' since their respective mean scores are 3.2145 and 3.0819. Regarding the view on the variables in domestic support, the significant difference among the employees in PSBs and PRBs have been noticed in the case of 'my family members take care my children', 'family members help me during financial crisis', 'frequent participation with my family members and friends', and 'I always have my family members who care for me' since their respective 't' statistics are significant at five per cent level.

Score on Domestic Support (SDS) among the Employees

The scores of the six variables related to domestic support among the employees have been included for the reliability analysis. The reliability co-efficient (0.7904) indicates that the included six variables explain it to the extent of 79.04 per cent. The SDS of the employees in the present study is confined to less than 2.00; 2.00 to 3.00; 3.01 to 4.00 and above 4.00. The distribution of employees on the basis of their SDS is given in Table 3.22.

Table 3.22: Score on domestic support (SDS) among the employees

Sl.No.	SDS	Number of Employees in		Total
		PSBs	PRBs	
1.	Less than 2.00	62(20)	6(5.40)	68(16.15)
2.	2.00 - 3.00	114(36.77)	74(66.67)	188(44.66)
3.	3.01 - 4.00	108(34.84)	22(19.82)	130(30.88)
4.	Above 4.00	26(8.39)	9(8.11)	35(8.31)
	Total	**310(100)**	**111(100)**	**421(100)**
Reliability co-efficient: 0.7904.				

Note: Figures in brackets indicate percentage

The important SDS among the employees are 2.00 to 3.00 and 3.01 to 4.00 which constitute 44.66 and 30.88 per cent of their respective totals. The employees with the SDS of above 4.00 constitute 8.31 per cent of the total respondents. The important SDS among the employees in PSBs are 2.00 to 3.00 and 3.01 to 4.00 which constitute 36.77 and 34.84 per cent of their respective totals. Among the employees in PRBs these are also 2.00 to 3.00 and 3.01 to 4.00 which constitute 66.67 and 19.82 per cent of their respective totals. The analysis infers that the SDS among the employees in PSBs is greater than that among the employees in PRBs.

SUPPORT FROM SUPERVISORS

One of the work-related support factors is 'support from supervisors'. The support from supervisor is inevitable to maintain the work-life balance among the employees. In the present study, 'the support from supervisor' has been measured with the help of six variables which are measured at five point scale. The mean scores of the variable 'support from supervisors' among the employees in PSBs and PRBs have been computed separately to exhibit the level of support among them. The 't' test has been used to find out the difference among the employees in PSBs and PRBs regarding their view on the variable 'support from supervisors'. The results are given in Table 3.23.

Table 3.23: Support from supervisors (SFS)

Sl. No.	Variables in SFS	Mean Score among the Employees in		't' statistics
		PSBs	PRBs	
1.	Supervisor is always helping minded	3.6244	2.5149	3.1456*
2.	Supervisor extends his support at the critical time of work	3.3081	2.4021	2.8091*
3.	Superior understands my problem	3.4653	2.9956	1.7376
4.	Supervisor is a participative type	3.8234	3.0149	2.7334*
5.	Supervisor provides a flexible schedule for me	3.7079	2.9091	2.8145*
6.	Supervisor is highly generous	3.7344	3.0114	2.5165*

** Significant at five per cent level.*

The highly viewed variables in SFS among the employees in PSBs are 'supervisor is a participative type' and 'supervisor is highly generous' since their mean scores are 3.8234 and 3.7344 respectively. Among the employees in PRBs, these two variables are 'supervisor is participative type' and 'supervisor is highly generous' since their mean scores are 3.0149 and 3.0114 respectively. Regarding the perception on the variables in SFS, the significant differences among the employees in the two groups of banks have been identified in the case of all variables except 'supervisor understands my problem' since its 't' statistics is not significant at five per cent level.

Score on Support from Supervisors (SSFS)

The scores of six variables of SFS have been included for the reliability analysis. The reliability co-efficient (0.8244) represents that the included 6 variables in 'support from supervisors' explain it to the extent of 82.44 per cent level. The SSFS among the employees in the present study, is confined to less than 2.00; 2.00 to 3.00; 3.01 to 4.00 and above 4.00. The distribution of employees on the basis of their SSFs is given in Table 3.24.

Table 3.24: Score on support from supervisors (SSFS)

Sl.No.	SSFS	Number of Employees in		Total
		PSBs	PRBs	
1.	Less than 2.00	64(20.65)	9(8.11)	73(17.34)
2.	2.00-3.00	74(23.87)	62(55.86)	136(32.30)
3.	3.01-4.00	114(36.77)	29(26.13)	143(33.97)
4.	Above 4.00	58(18.71)	11(9.90)	69(16.39)
	Total	**310(100)**	**111(100)**	**421(100)**
Reliability co-efficient: 0.8244				

Note: Figures in brackets indicate percentage

The important SSFS among the employees is 3.01 to 4.00 and 2.00 to 3.00 which constitute 33.97 and 32.30 per cent of the respective totals. The employees with the SSFS of above 4.00 constitute 16.39 per cent of the total. The important SSFS among the employees in PSBs are 3.01 to 4.00 and 2.00 to 3.00 which constitutes 36.77 and 23.87 per cent of their respective total. Among the employees in PRBs, these two SSFS are 2.00 to 3.00 and 3.01 to 4.00 which constitute 55.86 and 26.13 per cent of their respective total. The analysis reveals that the SSFS among the employees in PSBs is greater than that among the employees in PRBs.

SUPPORT FROM CO-WORKERS

The important factor of work-related support to employees, is the support from co-workers. The support gives by the co-workers may reduce the work-life imbalance among the employees. Hence it is included as one of the variables. The support from co-workers among the employees, has been measured with the help of seven variables. The employees are asked to rate these variables at five point scale. The mean scores of the variables among the employees in PSBs and PRBs have been computed separately, in order to exhibit the level of support from the co-workers. The results are given in Table 3.25

Table 3.25: Support from co-worker (SFC)

Sl. No.	Variables in SFC	Mean Score among the Employees in		't' statistics
		PSBs	PRBs	
1.	Co-workers are highly adjustable	3.2456	2.3452	2.9196*
2.	Co-workers are highly supportive	3.3919	2.6196	2.9344*
3.	Co-workers share my responsibilities during emergency	3.7345	2.7085	3.0149*
4.	Co-workers are highly informative	3.8142	2.9334	2.5038*
5.	Team spirit among the co-workers	3.6049	2.6885	2.6336*
6.	Co-workers are taking risks on behalf of me	3.6644	2.3036	3.4514*
7.	Co-worker are always sharing their work and life experiences	3.4586	2.4549	2.9909*

* *Significant at five per cent level.*

The highly viewed variables in SFC among the employees in PSBs are 'co-workers are highly informative' and 'co-workers share my responsibilities during emergency' since their mean scores are 3.8142 and 3.7345 respectively. Among the employees in PRBs, these two are also the same but with the different mean scores of 2.9334 and 2.7085 respectively. Regarding the perception on the variables related to SFC, the significant difference among the employees in PSBs and PRBs has been noticed in all seven variables in SFC since their respective 't' statistics are significant at five per cent level.

Score on Support from Co-workers (SSFC)

Seven variables have been included to explain the support from co-workers among the employees. The reliability co-efficient (0.8648) represents that the included seven variables in the SFC explain it to the extent of 86.48 per cent. The score of the SFC is computed by the mean scores of the variables in SFC. The scores, on SFC among the employees, in the present study, are confined to less than 2.00; 2.00 to 3.00 and 3.01 to 4.00. The distribution of employees on the basis of their SSFC is shown in Table 3.26.

Table 3.26: Score on support from co-workers (SSFC)

Sl.No.	Variables	Number of Employees in		Total
		PSBs	PRBs	
1.	Less than 2.00	50(16.13)	16(14.41)	66(15.68)
2.	2.00 - 3.00	65(20.97)	68(61.26)	133(31.59)
3.	3.01 - 4.00	129(41.61)	19(17.12)	148(35.15)
4.	Above 4.00	66(21.29)	8(7.21)	74(17.58)
	Total	**310(100)**	**111(100)**	**421(100)**
Reliability co-efficient: 0.8648.				

Note: Figures in brackets indicate percentage

The dominant SSFC among the employees are 3.01 to 4.00 and 2.00 to 3.00 which constitute 35.15 and 31.59 per cent of their respective totals. The employees with the SSFC of above 4.00 constitute 17.58 per cent of the total. The important SSFC among the employees in PSBs are 3.01 to 4.00 and above 4.00 which constitute 41.61 and 21.29 per cent of their respective total. Among the employees in PRBs, these two are 2.00 to 3.00 and 3.01 to 4.00 which constitute 61.26 and 17.12 per cent of their respective total. The SSFC among the employees in PSBs is higher than that among the employees in PRBs.

COMPARATIVE ANALYSIS ON SOCIAL SUPPORT AMONG THE EMPLOYEES

The 'social support' is classified into spouse support, domestic support, support from supervisors and support from co-workers. The mean scores of above said four categories of social supports among the employees in PSBs and PRBs have been computed separately, in order to exhibit the social support among the employees. Regarding the four categories of social supports, the significant difference among the employees in PSBs and PRBs have been analysed with the help of 't' test. The results are presented in Table 3.27.

Table 3.27: Comparative analysis on the social support among the employees

Sl. No.	Social Support	Mean Score among the Employees in		't' statistics
		PSBs	PRBs	
1.	Spouse support	3.6678	3.0596	2.0144*
2.	Domestic support	3.4085	2.8484	2.3617*
3.	Support from supervisors	3.6106	2.8080	2.9034*
4.	Support from co-worker	3.5592	2.5791	3.8969*

** Significant at five per cent level.*

In all four social supports, the employees in PSBs have more perception on the supports than the employees in PRBs. Regarding the four categories of social supports, the significant difference among the employees in PSBs and PRBs has been identified since their respective 't' statistics are significant at five per cent level. The highly perceived social support by the employees of PSBs is 'spouse support' since its mean score is 3.6678 whereas among the employees of PRBs, it is also the same but with the mean score of 3.0596.

Work-life Imbalance and Its Antecedents

INTRODUCTION

Work and family conflicts have emerged as an increasingly important research topic during the last few decades. According to Zedeck (1992),[1] this phenomenon is partly, due to the increase in the number of women employees in the work place, the changing attitudes towards work and the changing roles of family members. Further more, today's work place is increasingly populated with working parents, single parents, and dual-career couples (Thomas and Hauster, 1995).[2] The potential for work-family conflict increases as these working parents or dual couples struggle with the everyday work and home responsibilities. More than 50 per cent of work force is married with children, which suggests that information about this group is extremely relevant for strategic human resource management and exployees (Duxlury and Higgins, 1991).[3]

Studies have investigated the antecedents of work-family conflict. (Frone *et al.* 1997;[4] Frone and Yardley, 1996).[5] According to them, the more hours an individual spends on roles associated with work and/or family domains, role stress, role overload, social support, job complexity., career development issues and job security are the important antecedents of work-family interface.

The work family interface results from incompatible work and family demands (Kopelam *et al.* 1983).[6] There are two forms of work and family conflicts namely Work Interference with Family (WIF) and Family Interference with Work (FIW) (Gutek *et al.* 1991).[7]

Work can interfere with family when work demands prevent the fulfillment of family demands. Family can interfere with work when family demands prevent the fulfillment of work demands.

In the present study, the antecedents of Work-family Conflict and Family-work Conflict have been examined with the help of organizational role stressors and work domain variables.

ROLE STRESS

Human behaviour, in an organization, is influenced by various physical, social and psychological factors. An important aspect of organization that integrates an individual with the organization, is the role assigned to her within the overall structure of the organization. It is through this role, that an individual interacts and becomes integrated with the system. In fact, an organization can be defined as the system of roles. Kahn *et al.* (1964)[8] in their 'Comprehensive and integrated model of stress', postulated that the quest for identity is a central concern for many individuals. They considered a specific type of stress, in the form of role stress. Constructs like the conflict, role ambiguity, and role overload were put under role stress.

Even though, the 'Organizational Role stress Scale' (ORS) developed by Pareek (1983)[9] consists of two role stressors, the present study confines it to lack of role autonomy, role ambiguity, role conflict and role overload since these are most appropriate to estimate the antecedents of work life balance among the woman employees in banking industry (Pareek, 1997).[10]

Lack of Role Autonomy

It represents the lack of role autonomy to the woman employees in the organization regarding decision making on any relevant issue. Sometimes, this role of autonomy may lead to work-life imbalance among the employees. Hence, it is included as one of the variables in the present study. The lack of role autonomy among the employees, in the present study, is measured with the help of six statements. The employees are asked to rate these, at five point scale according to the order of existence in their organization, from very high to very low. The mean scores of the variables among the employees in PSBs and PRBs have been computed, to show the level of lack of role autonomy among the employees in their banks.

Table 4.1: Statements on lack of role autonomy among the employees

Sl. No.	Statements on Lack of Role Autonomy	Mean Score among the Employees in		't' statistics
		PSBs	PRBs	
1.	I have no freedom to design my work schedule	3.0145	3.9263	-2.8648*
2.	I have no independence and responsibility in my work	2.7408	3.8445	-2.9639*
3.	Lesser personal responsibility in my work	2.6834	3.6456	-2.2144*
4.	I have no own procedures to be used in my work	2.9903	3.9093	-2.8065*
5.	I have no authority to allocate resources	3.0183	3.8042	-2.8142*
6.	Higher rigidity in my job	3.0242	3.9429	-2.9085*

* *Significant at five per cent level.*

Table 4.1 explains the mean of the variables in 'lack of autonomy among the employees' in PSBs and PRBs and its respective 't'' statistics. The highly viewed variables among the employees in PSBs are 'higher rigidity in the job' and 'no authority to allocate resources' since their mean scores are 3.0242 and 3.0183 respectively. Among the employees in PRBs, these variables are 'higher rigidity in the job' and 'no freedom to design the work schedule' since their mean scores are 3.9429 and 3.9263 respectively. Regarding the perception on these variables, the significant differences among the two groups of employees have been noticed in the case of all six variables in 'lack of role autonomy' since their respective *'t'* statistics are significant at five per cent level.

Score on Lack of Role Autonomy (SLRA) among the Employees

The scores of the six variables related to 'lack of role autonomy' have been included for the reliability analysis. The reliability co-efficient (0.7901) indicates, that the included variable in 'lack of role autonomy' explains it to the extent of 79.01 per cent. The score on lack of role autonomy (SLRA) is confined to less than 2.00; 2.00 to 3.00; 3.01 to 4.00 and above 4.00. The distribution of employees on the basis of SLRA is shown in Table 4.2.

Table 4.2: Score on lack of role autonomy among the employees

Sl.No.	SLRA	Number of Employees in		Total
		PSBs	PRBs	
1.	Less than 2.00	59(19.03)	9(8.11)	68(16.16)
2.	2.00 – 3.00	184(59.35)	21(18.92)	205(48.69)
3.	3.01 – 4.00	49(15.81)	47(42.34)	96(22.80)
4.	Above 4.00	18(5.81)	34(30.63)	52(12.35)
	Total	**310(100)**	**111(100)**	**421(100)**
Reliability co-efficient: 0.7901.				

Note: Figures in brackets indicate percentage

The important SLRA among the employees are 2.00 to 3.00 and 3.01 to 4.00 which constitute 48.69 and 22.80 per cent of their respective totals. The employees with the SLRA of above 4.00 constitute 12.35 per cent of the total. The important SLRA among the employees in PSBs are 2.00 to 3.00 and less than 2.00 which constitute 59.35 and 19.03 per cent of their respective totals. Among the employees in PRBs, these two are 3.01 to 4.00 and above 4.00 which constitute 42.34 and 30.63 per cent of their respective total. The analysis reveals that 'lack of role autonomy' is identified as higher among the employees in PRBs than among the employees in PSBs.

Role Ambiguity among the Employees

The unclarity of duties and responsibilities, assigned to the employees may also lead to work-life imbalance. Hence, the role ambiguity has been included as one of the role stress factors in the present study. The role ambiguity among the employees in the present study is measured with the help of six variables which are measured at five point scale, from very high to very low, according to the order of existence in their banks. The mean scores of the variables in role ambiguity among the employees in PSBs and PRBs have been computed separately to exhibit the level of role ambiguity among the employees. The *'t'* test has been executed to find out the significant difference among the two groups of employees, regarding their level of role ambiguity. The results are shown in Table 4.3.

Table 4.3: Variables in role ambiguity among the employees

Sl. No.	Variables in Role Ambiguity	Mean Score among the Employees in		't' statistics
		PSBs	PRBs	
1.	Lack of clarity of scope and responsibility in the job	3.2708	3.7453	-2.1403*
2.	No established procedure in my job	2.9969	3.4081	-2.0144*
3.	My role in the work is vague	3.1411	3.6562	-2.0331*
4.	Lack of facts and information given to me about my work	2.7034	3.7141	-3.4509*
5.	Not knowing the level of expectation of authorities	3.0593	3.8462	-3.0412*
6.	My role has been reduced to nothing	2.8184	3.6563	-2.8919*

**Significant at five per cent level.*

The highly viewed role ambiguity variables among the employees in PSBs are 'Lack of clarity of scope and responsibility in the job' and 'vagueness of role in the work' since their respective mean scores are 3.2708 and 3.1411 respectively. Among the employees in PRBs, these two variables are 'not knowing the level of expectation of authorities' and 'Lack of clarity of scope and responsibility in the job' since their respective mean scores are 3.8462 and 3.7453 respectively. Regarding the perception on variables in role ambiguity, the significant differences among the two groups of employees have been noticed in all six variables, since their respective *'t'* statistics are significant at five per cent level.

Score on Role Ambiguity (SRA) among the Employees

The level of role ambiguity among the employees has been measured with the help of six variables. The reliability of the six variables in role ambiguity has been examined with the help of Cronbach alpha. The results indicate that the included six variables explain it to the extent of 81.44 per cent since its reliability co-efficient is 0.8144. The score of role ambiguity (SRA) among the employees, in the present study, is confined to less than 2.00; 2.00 to 3.00; 3.01 to 4.00 and above 4.00. The distribution of employees on the basis of their SRA is given in Table 4.4.

Table 4.4: Score on role ambiguity among the employees

Sl.No.	SRA	Number of Employees in		Total
		PSBs	PRBs	
1.	Less than 2.0	69(22.26)	14(12.61)	83(19.72)
2.	2.00–3.00	95(30.65)	26(23.42)	121(28.74)
3.	3.01–4.00	98(31.61)	39(35.14)	137(32.54)
4.	Above 4.00	48(15.48)	32(28.83)	80(19)
	Total	**310(100)**	**111(100)**	**421(100)**
Reliability co-efficient: 0.8144.				

Note: Figures in brackets indicate percentage

The important SRAs among the employees are 3.01 to 4.00 and 2.00 to 3.00 which constitute 32.54 and 28.74 per cent of their respective total. The employees with the SRA of above 4.00 constitute 19.00 per cent of the total. The important SRAs among the employees in PSBs are 3.01 to 4.00 and 2.00 to 3.00 which constitute 31.61 and 30.65 per cent of their respective total. Among the employees in PRBs, these two SRAs are 3.01 to 4.00 and above 4.00 which constitute 35.14 and 28.83 per cent of their respective total. The analysis reveals that the level of role ambiguity is higher among the employees in PRBs than among the employees in PSBs.

Role Conflict among the Employees

The role conflict represents the conflict between the personal and organizational role and the actual and expected role of the employees. Since the role conflict has influence on the work life imbalance among the employees, it is included as one of the factors. In the present study, the role conflict among the employees has been measured with the help of six variables, which are measured at five point scale. The mean scores of the variables among the employees in PSBs and PRBs have been computed separately. The results are given in Table 4.5.

The highly viewed variables in role conflict among the employees in PSBs are 'incompatible instructions from several people' and 'do not work in my expected role' since their mean scores are 3.1129 and 3.0645 respectively. Among the employees in PRBs, these two

Table 4.5: Variables in role conflict among the employees

Sl. No.	Variables in Role Conflict	Mean Score among the Employees in		't' statistics
		PSBs	PRBs	
1.	I do not work in my expected role	3.0645	3.8184	-2.8184*
2.	Incompatible instructions from several people	3.1129	3.9026	-2.8302*
3.	My values conflict with the organization's values	2.8442	3.6562	-2.9029*
4.	The expectation of superiors conflict with those of mine	2.6068	3.4133	-2.5142*
5.	I am unable to satisfy the conflicting demands	2.6361	3.5092	-2.9691*
6.	I do things acceptable by a few but not others	3.0143	3.8645	-2.7074*

* *Significant at five per cent level.*

are 'incompatible instructions from several people' and 'do things acceptable by a few but not others' since their respective mean scores are 3.9026 and 3.8645 respectively. Regarding the perception on variables in role conflict, the significant differences among the two groups of employees have been noticed in the case of all six variables since their respective *'t'* statistics are significant at five per cent level.

Score on Role Conflict (SRC) among the Employees

The scores on the role conflict (SRC) of the employees, has been computed by the mean scores of the variables included in role conflict. The reliability co-efficient indicates that the included six variables in role conflict, explain it to the extent of 76.13 per cent. The SRC of the employees in the present study is confined to less than 2.00; 2.00 to 3.00; 3.01 to 4.00 and above 4.00. The distribution of employees on the basis of SRC is presented in Table 4.6. (*See table on next page*)

The important SRCs among the employees in the present study are 2.00 to 3.00 and 3.01 to 4.00 which constitute 36.34 and 29.69 per cent of their respective total. The employees with the SRC of above 4.00 constitute 21.14 per cent of the total. The important SRC

Table 4.6: Score on role conflict (SRC) among the employees

Sl.No.	SRC	Number of Employees in		Total
		PSBs	PRBs	
1.	Less than 2.00	42(13.55)	12(10.81)	54(12.83)
2.	2.00–3.00	134(43.23)	19(17.12)	153(36.34)
3.	3.01–4.00	76(24.52)	49(44.14)	125(29.69)
4.	Above 4.00	58(18.70)	31(27.93)	89(21.14)
	Total	**310(100)**	**111(100)**	**421(100)**
Reliability co-efficient: 0.7613.				

Note: Figures in brackets indicate percentage

among the employees in PSBs are 2.00 to 3.00 and 3.01 to 4.00 which constitute 43.23 and 24.52 per cent of their respective total. Among the employees in PRBs, these are 3.01 to 4.00 and above 4.00 which constitute 44.14 and 27.93 per cent of their respective total. The higher role conflict is identified among the employees in PRBs than those in PSBs.

Role Overload among the Employees

The heavy work load among the employees may affect the work-life balance of the employees. In the present study, the role overload among the employees has been computed with the help of six variables which are measured at five point scale. The mean scores of the variables, in role overload, among the employees in PSBs and PRBs have been computed to exhibit the level of role overload among the two groups of employees. The '*t*' test has been used to identify the significant difference among the two groups of employees regarding their perception on variables, in role overload. The results are shown in Table 4.7.

The highly perceived variables in role overload among the employees in PSBs are 'too many supervisory hours are imposed on me' and 'I feel over-burdened in the role' since their mean scores are 3.2446 and 3.2041 respectively. Among the employees in PRBs, these two are 'feeling overburdened in the role' and 'my job assignments are very much taxing' since their respective mean scores are 4.0914 and 3.9909. Regarding the perception on variables in role overload, the significant differences between the employees in PSBs and PRBs have been identified in the case of all six variables since their respective '*t*' statistics are significant at five per cent level.

Table 4.7: Variables in role overload among the employees

Sl. No.	Variables in Role Overload	Mean Score among the Employees in		't' statistics
		PSBs	PRBs	
1.	My work load is heavy	3.0662	3.9149	-3.1441*
2.	I have no sufficient assistance to complete my assignment	3.1145	3.9608	-2.8628*
3.	I feel over-burdened in my role	3.2041	4.0914	-2.7447*
4.	Much expectations rest on me	3.1911	3.8562	-2.7603*
5.	My job assignments are very much taxing	3.0145	3.9909	-3.1408*
6.	Too many supervisory hours are imposed on me	3.2446	3.9694	-2.5646*

* *Significant at five per cent level.*

Score on Role Overload (SRO) among the Employees

The level of role overload among the employees, has been derived from the mean scores of the variables in role overload. The six variables included in the role overload explain it to the extent of 82.04 per cent, since their respective reliability co-efficient is 0.8204. The score on role overload (SRO) among the employees is confined to less than 2.00; 2.00 to 3.00; 3.01 to 4.00 and above 4.00. The distribution of employees on the basis of their SRO is given in Table 4.8.

Table 4.8: Score on role overload (SRO) among the employees

Sl.No.	SRO	Number of Employees in		Total
		PSBs	PRBs	
1.	Less than 2.00	61(19.68)	12(10.81)	73(17.34)
2.	2.00 – 3.00	92(29.67)	20(18.02)	112(26.60)
3.	3.01 – 4.00	104(33.55)	45(40.54)	149(35.39)
4.	Above 4.00	53(17.10)	34(30.63)	87(20.67)
	Total	**310(100)**	**111(100)**	**421(100)**
Reliability co-efficient: 0.8204.				

Note: Figures in brackets indicate percentage

The important SROs among the employees are 3.01 to 4.00 and 2.00 to 3.00 which constitute 35.39 and 26.60 per cent of their respective total. The employees with the SROs of above 4.00 constitute 20.67 per cent of the total. The important SROs among the employees in PSBs are 3.01 to 4.00 and 2.00 to 3.00 which constitute 33.55 and 29.67 per cent of their respective total. Among the employees in PRBs, these two are 3.01 to 4.00 and above 4.00 which constitutes 40.54 and 30.63 of their respective total. The analysis reveals that the role overload among the employees in PRBs is higher than that among the employees in PSBs.

Comparative View on the Role Stresses

The role stresses in the present study is classified into lack of role autonomy, role ambiguity, role conflict and role overload. The scores on the four important role stresses have been computed by the mean score of variables in each role stress. The mean score of each important role stress has been computed to exhibit the level of role stress among the women employees in banks. Regarding the perception on the above said four role stresses, the significant differences among the employees in PSBs and PRBs, have been computed with the help of 't' test. The mean scores of the four role stresses among the employees in PSBs and PRBs; and the respective '*t*' statistics are given in Table 4.9.

Table 4.9: Comparative analysis on role stress among the employees in PSBs and PRBs

Sl. No.	Role Stress	Mean Score among the Employees in		'*t*' statistics
		PSBs	PRBs	
1.	Lack of role autonomy	2.9120	3.8455	-2.9041*
2.	Role ambiguity	2.9983	3.6710	-2.5149*
3.	Role conflict	2.8798	3.6940	-2.8647*
4.	Role overload	3.1392	3.9639	-2.6603*

** Significant at five per cent level.*

The highly viewed role stresses among the employees in PSBs are 'role overload' and 'role ambiguity' since their respective mean scores are 3.1392 and 2.9983. Among the employees in PRBs, these two are 'role overload' and 'lack of role autonomy' since their respective mean scores are 3.9639 and 3.8455. Regarding the role stresses, significant differences among the employees in PSBs and PRBs, have been noticed in all the four role stresses since their respective '*t*' statistics are significant at five per cent level. The level of role stresses among the employees in PRBs is higher than that among the employees in PSBs.

Association between Profile Variables and the Perception on Role Stress among the Employees

Since the profile of the employees may be associated with the employees' perception on role stresses, the present study has made an attempt to analyse it with the help of one way analysis of variance. The included profile variables are age, educational qualification, personal income and years of experience of the employees. The result of one-way analysis of variance is summarized in Table 4.10.

Table 4.10: Association between profile variables of employees and their perception on role stresses

Sl. No.	Profile Variables	F-statistics			
		Lack of Role Autonomy	Role Ambiguity	Role Conflict	Role Overload
1.	Age	2.6456*	1.8186	1.4189	2.8462*
2.	Educational qualification	2.6802*	2.8082*	2.7133*	1.9641
3.	Personal income	2.4317*	1.3011	2.5082*	2.0417
4.	Years of experience	2.8568*	1.0862	2.6817*	2.5624*

**Significant at five per cent level.*

Regarding the perception on lack of role autonomy, the significantly associating profile variables are age, educational qualification, personal income and years of experience since their respective 'F' statistics are significant at five per cent level. The profile variables that significantly associate with the perception on role ambiguity is educational qualification whereas in the perception on role conflict, these profile variables are educational qualification, personal income and years of experience. Regarding the perception on 'role overload', the variables that significantly associate are age and years of experience since their respective 'F' statistics are significant at five per cent level.

Association between Family Domain Variables and the Perception on Role Stresses

The family domain variables may have their own influence on the employees' perception on their role stresses. Hence, the present study has made an attempt to analyse the association with the help of one-way analysis of variance. The included family domain variables are marital status, type of family, family size, number of earning members per family, level of education of spouse, employment of spouse, parental status, age of the youngest child, family income, earning responsibilities and time devoted to family work per day. The results are given in Table 4.11.

Table 4.11: Association between family domain variables and employees' perception on role stresses

Sl. No.	Family Domain Variables	F-statistics			
		Lack of Role Autonomy	Role Ambiguity	Role Conflict	Role Overload
1.	Marital status	2.0142	2.1403	1.8942	1.9043
2.	Type of family	1.8567	2.9092	3.0033	3.5025
3.	Family size	2.5044*	2.0661	2.7871*	2.9145*
4.	Number of earning members per family	1.8911	2.9143*	2.6646*	3.1042*
5.	Level of education of spouse	2.5603*	2.7664*	1.8802	2.6044*
6.	Employment of spouse	2.0914	3.2144	3.7145	3.9647*
7.	Parental status	2.0911	3.9917*	3.9611*	3.9244*
8.	Age of the youngest child	1.8483	2.0451	2.3345	2.7681*
9.	Family income	2.5062*	2.7664*	2.9041*	3.0525*
10.	Caring responsibilities	2.5828*	2.6236*	2.9233*	2.8617*
11.	Time devoted to family work per day	1.8417	2.9103*	2.8217*	2.9217*

**Significant at five per cent level.*

Regarding the perception on lack of role autonomy, the significantly associating family domain variables are family size, level of education of spouse, family income and caring responsibilities since their respective 'F' statistics are significant at five per cent level. The family domain variables that significantly associate with the perception on role ambiguity are number of earning members per family, level of education of spouse, parental status, family income, caring responsibilities and time devoted to family work per day. Regarding the perception on 'role conflict', the significantly associating family domain variables are family size, number of earning member per family, parental status, family income, caring responsibilities and time devoted to family work per day whereas in the perception on 'role overload', these family domain variables are family size, number of earning members per family, level of education of spouse, employment of spouse, parental status, age of the youngest child, family income, caring responsibilities and time devoted to family work per day.

Discriminant Role Stressors among the Employees in PSBs and PRBs

The role stresses among the employees in PSBs and PRBs may be different in different degrees. In order to formulate some policy implications, it is imperative to identify the important discriminant role stresses among the two groups of employees. Initially, the mean difference in all the four role stresses and the discriminant power of the role stresses have been computed and presented in Table 4.12.

Table 4.12: Mean difference and discriminant power of stresses among the employees in PSBs and PRBs

Sl. No.	Role Stresses	Mean Scores among Employees in		Mean Difference	't' statistics	Wilks Lambda
		PSBs	PRBs			
1.	Lack of role autonomy (X_1)	2.9120	3.8455	-0.9335	-2.9041*	0.2583
2.	Role ambiguity (X_2)	2.9983	3.6710	-0.6727	-2.5149*	0.1411
3.	Role conflict (X_3)	2.8798	3.6940	-0.8142	-2.8647*	0.3455
4.	Role overload (X_4)	3.1392	3.9639	-0.8247	-2.6605*	0.1208

Significant mean difference is identified in all the four role stresses since their respective 't' statistics are significant at five per cent level. Higher mean differences are identified in the case of 'lack of role autonomy' and 'role overload' since their respective mean differences are -0.9335 and -0.8247 respectively. The higher discriminant power of the role stresses is identified in the case of 'role overload' and 'role ambiguity' since their respective Wilk's Lambda are 0.1208 and 0.1411. The significant role stresses are included to estimate the two group discriminant function. The unstandardised procedure has been followed to estimate the function. The estimated function is:

$$Z = -1.2344 - 0.0473X_1 - 0.2453X_2 - 0.2865X_3 - 0.3861X_4$$

The relative contribution of discriminant role stresses in total discriminant score (TDS) has been calculated by the product of the discriminant co-efficient and the respective mean difference of the role stresses. The results are given in Table 4.13.

Table 4.13: Relative contribution of discriminant role stresses in total discriminant score (TDS)

Sl. No.	Role Stresses	Discriminant Co-efficient	Mean Difference	Product	Relative Contribution in TDS
1.	Lack of role autonomy	-0.0473	-0.9335	0.0442	5.81
2.	Role ambiguity	-0.2453	-0.6727	0.1650	21.68
3.	Role conflict	-0.2865	-0.8142	0.2333	30.66
4.	Role overload	-0.3861	-0.8247	0.3184	41.85
	Total			**0.7609**	**100.00**
Per cent of cases correctly classified: 71.09					

The higher discriminant co-efficient is identified in the cases of 'role overload' and 'role conflict' since their discriminant co-efficients are -0.3861 and -0.2865 respectively. It represents higher degree of influence of the above two role stresses on the discriminant function. The higher relative contribution in TDS is noticed in the cases of 'role overload' and 'role conflict' since their contributions are 41.85 and 30.66 per cent respectively. The estimated function correctly classifies the cases to the extent of 71.09 per cent. The analysis reveals that the important discriminant role stresses among the employees in PSBs and PRBs are 'role overload' and 'role conflict' and these two are very high among the employees in PRBs when compared to those in PSBs.

WORK DOMAIN VARIABLES AMONG THE EMPLOYEES

The variables related to the working conditions, work content, working climate, inter-personal relationship and inter relationship between various departments are highly associating with the work-life interface among the employees. The employees who are having a better working climate and culture may have less degrees of work-family and family-work conflicts which are directly connected with the performance of the employees. Hence, the present study includes the work domain variables in the per cent study as one of the antecedents of work-family conflict. Even though, the work domain variables are too many, the present study is confined to only 30 variables.

The employees are asked to rate the 30 variables related to working domain, at five point scale, according to the order of existence in their banks namely very high, high, moderate, low and very low. The assigned marks on these scales are from 5 to 1 respectively. The mean scores of the variables in work domain have been computed among the employees in PSBs and PRBs, separately, to exhibit the level of existence of work domain. In order to find out the significant difference among the two groups of employees, the *'t'* test has been executed. The results are presented in Table 4.14.

Table 4.14: Mean score of work domain variables

Sl. No.	Work Domain Variables	Mean Score among Employees in		't' statistics
		PSBs	PRBs	
1	2	3		4
1.	My colleagues do not help in my the day to-day work plan	3.2845	3.9184	-2.2183*
2.	Inadequate Salary	2.7331	3.5648	-2.0644*
3.	Pressure on improved performance	3.1443	3.4145	-0.8087
4.	My bank do not provide enough opportunities to me	3.1049	3.8299	-2.2996*
5.	My colleagues do not help me in achieving the targets	3.4085	3.1142	0.3491
6.	No authority for decision-making in day to-day affairs	3.2917	3.8187	-2.0473*

Contd...

1	2	3		4
7.	No balance between my talents and salary	3.8404	3.2418	1.9988*
8.	Frequent change in Bank policies	3.2924	3.5663	-0.5092
9.	My colleagues are not trust-worthy	2.9079	3.8617	-2.6187*
10.	Dumping of heavy work load	3.2663	3.9942	-2.2408*
11.	Sharing of job with colleagues affects my own performance	2.8411	3.1908	-0.4419
12.	No proper acceptance of employees' request	3.6914	3.7562	-0.1332
13.	Poor empowerment in all aspects	3.4405	3.9245	-1.0917
14.	Monotony of repeated work	3.0124	3.9907	-2.6165*
15.	My colleagues are not supportive	2.5508	3.6618	–2.7341*
16.	Lack of recognition	2.6517	3.7379	-2.5866*
17.	Inconvenient working hours	2.4508	3.9984	-3.1446*
18.	Busy on the job activities in holidays also	2.6673	3.8997	-2.9445*
19.	No standardized working hours	2.4508	3.6637	-2.8184*
20.	Inadequate provision of resources to perform better	3.0213	3.2541	-0.2732*
21.	Undedicated supervisors	3.2057	3.7139	-1.3097
22.	Continuous review of workload	2.7134	3.0917	-0.3914
23.	No scope for career development	2.6629	3.5128	-2.4582*
24.	Inflexibility of working hours	2.9028	3.2834	-0.6822
25.	Inadequate incentives	3.0142	3.8817	-2.7339*
26.	Information overload	3.2646	3.8991	-2.2301*
27.	Lack of Independence	2.6703	3.8186	-3.5149*
28.	No job security	3.0911	3.7087	-1.9908*
29.	Poor working conditions	3.1442	2.9908	0.3168
30.	No clear cut duties and responsibilities	2.6634	3.7176	-2.3694*

** Significant at five per cent level.*

The highly viewed work domain variables among the employees in PSBs are 'no balance between my talents and salary' and 'poor empowerment in all aspects' since their respective mean scores are 3.8404 and 3.4405. Among the employees in PRBs, these are 'inconvenient working hours' and 'dumping of heavy work load' since their respective mean scores are 3.9984 and 3.9942. The less viewed work domain variables among the employees in PSBs are 'inconvenient working hours' and 'no standardized working hours' since their respective mean scores are 2.4508 and 2.4508. Among the employees in PRBs, the less perceived work domain variables are 'poor working conditions' and 'continues review of work load' since their respective mean scores are 2.9908 and 3.0917.

Regarding the perception on the work domain variables, the significant difference among the employees in PSBs and PRBs has been noticed in the case of 'my colleagues do not help in day to day work plan', 'inadequate salary', 'my bank do not provide enough opportunities to me', 'no authority for decision making on day-to-day affairs', 'no balance between my talents and salary', 'my colleagues are not trustworthy', 'dumping heavy work load', 'monotony of repeated work', 'my colleagues are not supportive', 'lack of recognition', 'inconvenient working hours', 'busy on the job activities in holidays also', 'no standardized working hours', 'inadequate provision of resources to perform better', 'no scope for career development', 'inadequate incentives', 'information overload',' lack of independence', 'no job security' and 'no clear cut duties and responsibilities' since their respective *'t'* statistics are significant at five per cent level.

Work Domain Factors among the Employees

In order to narrate the work domain variables into work domain factors, the Exploratory Factor Analysis (EFA) has been executed. Initially, the test of validity of data for factor analysis was conducted by Kaiser-Meyer-Ohlin (KMO) and then measure of sampling adequacy and Bartletts test of Sphercity. The minimum threshold of KMO measure is 0.50 per cent level. The scores of the thirty work domain variables have been included for the analysis. Since the KMO measure of sampling adequacy is 0.8634 and the level of significance of chi-square value is at zero per cent level, the validity of data for analysis has been confirmed. The EFA has been executed to narrate the work domain variables into factors. The result of EFA is presented in Table 4.15.

Table 4.15: Important work domain factors

Sl. No.	Work Domain Factors	Number of Variables	Reliability Co-efficient	Eigen Value	Percent of Variation Explained	Cumulative Per cent of Variation Explained
1.	Unsupportive colleagues	5	0.8437	4.0108	15.64	15.64
2.	Work pressure	5	0.7398	3.6667	12.34	27.98
3.	Performance Inhibitors	5	0.8248	3.1287	11.27	39.25
4.	Lack of Empowerment	5	0.6974	2.4642	10.68	49.93
5.	Effort reward imbalance	4	0.7911	2.1737	9.38	59.31
6.	Working hours	3	0.6974	1.3399	8.59	67.90
7.	Working conditions	3	0.7989	1.2344	7.45	75.35
	Total	**30**				
KMO measure of sampling Adequacy: 0.8142				Bartletts Test Sphericity Chi-square* value:89.17		

* *Significant at zero per cent level.*

The EFA have identified seven work domain factors namely unsupportive colleagues, pressure on work, performance inhibitors, lack of empowerment, effort-reward imbalance, working hours and working conditions. All the seven factors explain the work-domain variables to the extent of 75.35 per cent. The most important work domain factor identified by the factor analysis is 'unsupportive colleagues' since its eigen value and the per cent of variation explained is 4.0108 and 15.64 per cent respectively. It consists of five variables with the reliability co-efficient of 0.8437. It reveals that the included five variables in unsupportive colleagues explain it to the extent of 84.37 per cent.

The second and third important work domain factors are 'pressure on work' and 'performance inhibitors' since their eigen values are 3.6667 and 3.1287 respectively. The above said two factors consist of 5 variables each with the reliability co-efficient of 0.7398 and 0.8248 respectively. The next two work domain factors identified by the factor analysis are 'lack of empowerment' and 'effort-reward imbalance' since their factors consist of 5 and 4 variables with the reliability co-efficient of 0.6974 and 0.7911 respectively. The last two factors identified by the factor analysis are 'working hours' and 'working conditions' since their eiger values are 1.3399 and 1.2344 respectively. The above two factors consist of three variables each with the reliability co-efficient of 0.6974 and 0.7089 respectively. The EFA results in seven important factors for further analysis.

Reliability Validity Variables in each Work Domain Factor

The variables included in the work domain factors vary from 5 to 3. The scores of the variables included in each factor have been examined to confirm the reliability and validity of variables in each factor. The Confirmatory Factor Analysis (CFA) has been administered to test the reliability and validity of variables in each factor. The standardized factor loading of the variables, its '*t*' statistics, composite reliability and average variance extracted by each factor have been computed. The results are given in Table 4.16.

Table 4.16: Result of confirmatory factor analysis

Sl. No.	Work Domain Factors	Range of Standardized Factor Loading	Range of '*t*' statistics	Composite Reliability	Average Variance Extracted
1.	Unsupportive colleagues	0.9107 0.6832	4.1433* 2.9017*	0.8145	58.08
2.	Work pressure	0.8943 0.7145	3.8627* 3.1441*	0.7244	52.92
3.	Performance Inhibitors	0.9241 0.6407	4.2916* 2.4322*	0.7963	56.31
4.	Lack of empowerment	0.8404 0.6268	3.3491* 2.2108*	0.6723	51.04
5.	Effort reward imbalance	0.9036 0.6099	3.9044* 2.1436*	0.7309	53.17
6.	Working hours	0.8861 0.5944	3.7033* 2.0041*	0.6502	50.09
7.	Working conditions	0.8508 0.6503	3.5023* 2.6582*	0.7336	54.09

* *Significant at five per cent level.*

The *'t'* statistics of standardized factor loading of all variables, included in each work domain factor, is significant at five per cent level. It reveals the convergent validity of the factor. It is also confirmed by the composite reliability and average variance, extracted by the factor, since their respective composite reliability and average variance, extracted by the factor, are greater than the minimum threshold of 0.50 and 50.00 per cent respectively.

Perception on Work Domain Factors among the Employees

The employees' perception on work domain factors has been examined with the help of the mean scores of the work domain variables in each work domain factor. In the present study, there are seven work domain factors namely unsupportive colleagues, work pressure, performance inhibitors, lack of empowerment, effort-reward imbalance, working hours and working conditions. The mean scores of the above said seven work domain factors have been computed from the scores of work domain variables in each factor. The mean scores of the work domain factors among the employees in PSBs and PRBs have been computed separately. Regarding the existence of work domain factors, the significant mean differences in PSBs and PRBs have been examined with the help of *'t'* test. The results are presented in Table 4.17.

Table 4.17: Mean score of work domain factors among the employees

Sl. No.	Work Domain Factors	Mean Score among Employees in		't' statistics
		PSBs	PRBs	
1.	Unsupportive colleagues	2.8576	3.8148	-2.1245*
2.	Work Pressure	3.0631	3.9332	-1.9906*
3.	Performance Inhibitors	2.9879	3.7899	-2.0453*
4.	Lack of Empowerment	3.2109	3.8627	-2.1476*
5.	Effort-reward imbalance	2.8821	3.4855	-1.9989*
6.	Working hours	2.6115	3.6486	-2.7817*
7.	Working conditions	2.9662	3.3724	-1.2517

* *Significant at five per cent level.*

The highly viewed work domain factors among the employees in PSBs are 'work pressure' and 'lack of empowerment' since their respective mean scores are 3.0631 and 3.2109. Among the employees in PRBs, these two work domain factors are 'work pressure' and 'lack of empowerment' since their mean scores are 3.9332 and 3.8627 respectively. Regarding the perception on work domain factors, the significant differences among the employees in PSBs and PRBs have been noticed in the case of unsupportive colleagues, work pressure, performance inhibitors, lack of empowerment, effort-reward imbalance and working hours since their respective *'t'* statistics are significant at five per cent level.

Association between Profile Variables of Employees and their Work Domain Factors

Since the profile variables namely age, educational qualification, personal income and years of experience may be associated with the employees' perception on work domain factors, the present study has made an attempt to analyse such association, with the help of one way analysis of variance. The associations between control variables and the perception on seven work domain factors have been separately analysed. The result of the analysis of variances is given in Table 4.18.

Table 4.18: Association between profile variables of employees and their perception on work domain factors (WDF)

Sl. No.	Profile Variables	F-statistics						
		Unsupportive Colleagues	Pressure of Work	Performance Inhibitors	Lack of Empowerment	Effort Reward Imbalance	Working Hours	Working Conditions
1.	Age	2.8541*	2.9146*	3.1645*	1.0661	1.1019	2.8681*	1.9082
2.	Educational Qualification	2.7617*	2.8084*	2.1085	2.8566*	1.8445	2.0962	2.4599*
3.	Personal Income	2.4041*	1.3342	2.6942*	2.6591*	2.1141	2.0643	2.5759*
4.	Years of experience	2.6559*	1.0411	1.8969	2.8618*	2.8103*	2.5414*	1.8084

* *Significant at five per cent level.*

Regarding the perception on 'unsupportive colleagues', the significantly associating profile variables are age, educational qualification, personal income and years of experience since their respective 'F' statistics are significant at per cent level. Regarding the perception on 'pressure of work' the significantly associating profile variables are age and educational qualification of employees. The significantly associating profile variables with the perception of 'performance inhibitors' are age and personal income. Since their respective F-statistics are significant at five per cent level. The significantly associating control variables with the perception on 'lack of empowerment' are educational qualification, personal income and years of experience whereas regarding the perception on 'effort-reward imbalance', the significant control variable is year of experience only. In the perception on 'working hours', the significantly associating profile variables are age and years of experience whereas regarding the perception on 'working conditions', these profile variables are educational qualification and personal income. The analysis reveals the importance of age, education qualification, personal income and years of experience in the perception on the work domain factors.

Association between Family Domain Variables of the Employees and their Perception on WDFs

The identified family domain variables in the present study are marital status, type of family, family size, number of earning members per family, level of education of spouse, parental status, age of the youngest child, family income, caring responsibilities and time devoted to family work per day. The association between the above said family domain variables of the employees and their perception on the seven WDFs has been analysed, with the help of one way analysis of variance. The results are presented in Table 4.19.

The family domain variables that significantly associate with the view of 'unsupportive colleagues' are family size, level of education of spouse, employment of spouse, parental status, age of the youngest child, family income, caring responsibilities and time devoted to family work per day since their respective 'F' statistics are significant at five per cent level. Regarding the perception on 'pressure on work', the significantly associating family domain variable are marital status, family size, number of earning members per family, level of education of spouse, parental status, age of the youngest child, family income, caring responsibilities and time devoted to family work per day.

Table 4.19: Association between family domain variables and employees' perception on WDFs

Sl. No.	Family Domain Variables	F-statistics						
		Unsupportive Colleagues	Pressure of Work	Performance Inhibitors	Lack of Empowerment	Effort Reward Imbalance	Working Hours	Working Eonditions
1.	Marital status	2.3417	2.6818*	2.1448	2.3408	1.9945	2.8919*	29.134*
2.	Type of family	2.1408	3.0411	2.5617	3.1292	3.3414	3.5616	39.7142
3.	Family size	2.4563*	2.7314*	3.1408*	2.9104*	2.5632*	2.7314*	2.5041*
4.	Number of earning members per family	2.3408	2.6884*	2.9143*	2.0411	1.8908	2.2415	2.7314*
5.	Level of education of spouse	2.5344*	2.9102*	3.0144*	2.1414	1.6977	2.5142*	2.7029*
6.	Employment of spouse	3.9108*	3.1443	2.9142	3.2444	3.8144	2.8616	3.0814
7.	Parental status	3.9245*	3.9696*	2.0814	2.5657	2.8681	3.2345	3.7145
8.	Age of the youngest child	2.5657*	2.7332*	2.4542*	1.8991	2.0841	2.3381	2.6508*
9.	Family Income	2.5061*	2.5616*	1.9194	2.0568	2.3414	2.3678*	3.0414*
10.	Caring responsibilities	2.6544*	2.5053*	3.1408*	2.7121*	2.6166*	2.7331*	2.8166*
11.	Time devoted to family work per day	2.6016*	2.3919*	3.0891*	2.8616*	2.4514*	2.8184*	2.9021*

* *Significant at five per cent level.*

Regarding the perception on 'performance inhibitors', the significantly associating family domain variables are family size, number of earning members per family, level of education of spouse, age of the youngest child, caring responsibilities and time devoted to family work per day. The significantly associating family domain variables regarding the perception on 'lack of empowerment' and 'effort-reward imbalance' among the employees are family size, caring responsibilities and time devoted to family work per day. In the case of perception on 'working hours', these family domain variables are marital status, family size, level of education of spouse, family income, caring responsibilities and time devoted to family work per day whereas in the case of 'working conditions', these family domain variables are marital status, family size, number of earning members per family, level of education of spouse, age of the youngest child, family income, caring responsibilities and time devoted to family work per day, since their respective 'F' statistics are significant at five per cent level. The analysis reveals the importance of family domain variables namely family size, caring responsibilities and time devoted to family work per day in their perception on work domain factors among the employees in PSBs and PRBs.

Association between Organization Variables of the Employees and their Perception on WDFs

The identified organization variables, in the present study, are designation, hours worked per day and working schedule. The association between the above said three organization variables of the employees and their perception on seven work domain factors have been examined separately with the help of one way analysis of variance. The result of ANOVA is presented in Table 4.20.

The significantly associating organization variables, with the perception on 'unsupportive colleagues' among the employees are designation, hours worked per day and working schedule since their respective 'F' statistics are significant at five per cent level. Regarding the perception on 'pressure on work', the significantly associating organization variables are designation and hours worked per day. Regarding the perception on 'performance inhibitors', 'effort-reward imbalance', 'working hours' and 'working conditions', the significantly associating organization variables are hours worked per day and working schedule since their respective 'F' statistics are significant at five per cent level.

Table 4.20: Association between organization variables and the perception on WDFs among the employees

Sl. No.	Organization Variables	F-statistics						
		Unsupportive Colleagues	Pressure of Work	Performance Inhibitors	Lack of Empowerment	Effort Reward Imbalance	Working Hours	Working Conditions
1.	Designation	3.0824*	3.1445*	2.9492	2.5646	1.8969	2.3818	2.8616
2.	Hours worked per day	2.8184*	2.5084*	2.6887*	2.4107*	2.6633*	2.8185*	2.9196*
3.	Working schedule	3.1408*	2.4082	3.8144*	2.8602	2.9909*	3.1445*	3.2344*

* *Significant at five per cent level.*

Regarding the perception on 'lack of empowerment', the significantly associating organization variable is 'hours worked per day'. The analysis reveals the importance of hours worked per day and the perception on WDFs among the employees.

Discriminant Work Domain Variables among the Employees in PSBs and PRBs

The perception on work domain variables among the employees in PSBs and PRBs may differ since their nature, intensity and content of the works are different. It is imperative to analyse the important discriminant work domain variables among the employees among the two groups of banks for some policy implications. The two group discriminant analysis has been administered to identify such work domain variables. Initially, the mean difference and the discriminant power of the variables have been computed. The results are given in Table 4.21. (*See table on next page*)

The significant mean differences among the employees in PSBs and PRBs have been identified in the case of unsupportive colleagues, work pressure, performances inhibitors, lack of empowerment, effort-reward imbalance and working hours since their respective *'t'* statistics are significant at five per cent level. Higher mean difference is identified in the case of 'unsupportive colleagues' and 'working hours' since their mean differences are -0.9572 and -0.9571 respectively. Higher discriminant power of the variables is noticed in 'work pressure', 'working hours' and 'unsupportive colleagues' since their respective Wilk's Lambda co-efficient are 0.1026, 0.1143 and 0.1341.

Table 4.21: Mean difference and discriminant power of work domain variables among the employees in PSBs and PRBs

Sl. No.	Work Domain Variables	Mean Score among Employees		Mean Difference	't'-statistics	Wilk's Lambda
		PSBs	PRBs			
1.	Unsupportive colleagues	2.8576	3.8148	-0.9572	-2.1245*	0.1341
2.	Work pressure	3.0631	3.9332	-0.8701	-1.9906*	0.1026
3.	performance inhibitors	2.9879	3.7899	-0.8020	-2.0453*	0.3449
4.	Lack of empowerment	3.2109	3.8627	-0.6518	-2.1476*	0.1786
5.	Effort-reward imbalance	2.8821	3.4855	-0.6034	-1.8989*	0.5162
6.	Working hours	2.6915	3.6486	-0.9571	-2.7817*	0.1143
7.	Working conditions	2.9662	3.3724	-0.4062	-1.2517	0.6334

* *Significant at five per cent level.*

The significant work domain variables have been included for the two group discriminant analysis. The unstandardised procedure has been followed to identify the relative contribution of each discriminant variable in the total discriminant score. The fitted discriminant function is

$$Z = a+b_1x_1+b_2x_2+.............+b_nx_n$$

Where

Z	=	Discriminant criterion
$X_1........x_n$	=	Discriminant variables
$b_1,....b_n$	=	Discriminant co-efficients
a	=	Intercept

The relative contribution of each discriminant variable to the total discriminant score is computed by the product of unstandardised discriminant co-efficient and the mean difference of each discriminant variable. The results are given in Table 4.22.

Table 4.22: Relative contribution of discriminant work domain variables in total discriminant score (TDS)

Sl. No.	Discriminant Work Domain Variables	Unstandardized Discriminant Co-efficient	Mean Difference	Product	Relative Contribution in TDS
1.	Unsupportive colleagues	-0.1823	-0.9572	0.1745	18.73
2.	Pressure on work	-0.4182	-0.8701	0.3639	39.05
3.	Performance inhibitors	-0.0443	-0.8020	0.0355	3.81
4.	Lack of empowerment	-0.0965	-0.6518	0.0629	6.75
5.	Working hours	-0.3083	-0.9571	0.2951	31.66
	Total			**0.9319**	**100.00**
Per cent of cases correctly classified: 78.04.					

The higher discriminant co-efficient is noticed in the case of 'work pressure' and 'working hours' since their discriminant co-efficients are -0.4182 and -0.3083 respectively. It indicates higher influence of the above said two variables on the discriminant functions. Higher relative contribution in total discriminant score is identified in the cases of 'working pressures' and 'working hours' since their respective relative contributions are 39.05 and 31.66 per cent respectively. The estimated discriminant functions correctly classify the cases to the extent of 78.04 per cent. The analysis infers that 'work pressures' and 'working hours' are the important discriminant work domain variables which discriminate the employees in PSBs and PRBs. These two are very high among the employees in PRBs than among the employees in PSBs.

WORK-LIFE IMBALANCE AMONG THE EMPLOYEES

The work-life imbalance among the employees reflects in two ways namely work-family conflict and family-work conflict.

Work-family Conflict among the Employees

Work family conflict is a form of inter-role conflict in which role pressures from the work and family domains are incompatible in some respect (Greenhaus and Beutell, 1985).[11] Originally believed to be uni-dimensional, research in the area of work-family conflict, has recently focused on defining the conceptualization of work-family conflict (Carlson *et al.*, 2000[12] and Frone *et al.*, 1996).[13] Indeed, much of the past research concerning work-family conflict has failed to take into consideration the complex nature of the work-family issues. The work-family interface is also recognized as a presentable boundary. Demands at work, that interface with the family domain, have been found to be independent of demands within the family that interface with the work domain (Frone *et al.*, 1996). There are two dimensions of work-family conflict. These are time-based and strain-based. Time-based conflict occurs when time devoted to one role makes it difficult to participate in, or comply with the expectation of the other role. Strain-based conflict is viewed as strain from the demands of one role intruding into and interfering with the participation in another role.

The WFC among the employees, have been examined with the help of the mean score of the statements related to the WFC. The mean scores of the statements related to WFC among the employees in PSBs and PRBs have been computed separately. The 't' test has been applied to analyse the significant difference among the two groups of employees regarding the statements related to WFC.

Higher work-family conflict has been identified in the cases of 'stress leads to irritation at home' and 'work load keeps me away from my family activities' since their respective mean scores are 3.2818 and 3.2717 among the employees in PSBs. In the PRBs, higher work family conflict has been noticed in the cases of 'work affects the amount of time spent with family members' and 'work keeps the employees away from their family members' since their respective means scores are 4.1241 and 4.1027. Regarding the work-family conflict, the significant differences among the employees in PSBs and PRBs have been noticed in the case of all eight statements stated in Table 4.23. Since their respective 't' statistics are significant at five per cent level.

Table 4.23: Mean score on WFC among the employees

Sl. No.	Statements in WFC	Mean Score among Emmployees in		't' statistics
		PSBs	PRBs	
1.	I feel physically drained when I get home from work	3.2145	3.8679	-2.0452*
2.	Due to all pressure at work, when I come home I am too stressed to do the things I enjoy	3.0245	3.9197	-2.4514*
3.	My work often interferes with my family responsibilities	3.2144	3.9092	-2.2144*
4.	My work keeps me away from my family activities more than I would like to	3.2717	4.1027	-2.4545*
5.	The stress from my job often makes me irritable, when I get home	3.2818	3.9614	-2.0969*
6.	Due to role overload in the work, I am unable to meet my family members	2.8456	3.8147	-2.8503*
7.	My work affects the amount of time spent with my family members	3.1245	4.1241	-2.8399*
8.	Due to work pressure, I am unable to share my views with my family members	2.8345	3.6675	-2.0107*

* *Significant at five per cent level.*

Reliability and Validity of Statements in WFC

In the present study, the work family conflict (WFC) has been measured with the help of eight related statements. The respondents are asked to rate these statements at five per cent scale from highly agree to highly disagree. The assigned marks on these scales are from 5 to 1 respectively. The marks of the statements have been included for the confirmatory factor analysis of the reliability and validity of the construct namely work-family conflict. The result of the confirmatory factor analysis is given in Table 4.24.

Table: 4.24: reliability and validity of statements related to work-family conflict (WFC)

Sl. No.	Statements	Standardized Factor Loading	't' statistics	Composite Reliability Extracted	Average Variance	Reliability Co-efficient
1.	I feel physically drained when I get home from work	0.6993	3.2144*	0.8244	60.47	0.7204
2.	Due to all pressure at work, When I come home, I am too stressed to do things I enjoy	0.7224	3.3942*			
3.	My work often interferes with my family responsibilities	0.7607	4.2193*			
4.	My work keeps me away from my family activities more than I would like to	0.8149	5.2242*			
5.	The stress from my job often make me irritable when I get home	0.8334	5.6107*			
6.	Due to role overload in the work, I am unable to meet my family members	0.6883	3.0143*			
7.	My work affects the amount of time spent with my family members	0.7331	3.5063*			
8.	Due to work pressure, I am unable to share my views with my family members	0.8594	6.0337*			

* *Significant at five per cent level.*

Since the standardized factor loading and its 't' statistics are significant at five per cent level, the convergent validity of the construct is confirmed. The content validity of the construct has been proved since the average variance extracted by the construct is greater than the minimum threshold of 0.5. The composite reliability co-efficient is also greater than 0.5 which confirms the convergent validity. The reliability co-efficient reveals that the included eight statements in WFC explain the WFC to the extent of 72.04 per cent. Hence the eight statements have been included to measure the WFC among the executives in the present study.

Score on Work-family Conflict

The scores on work-family conflict among the employees have been measured with the help of the mean score of eight variables included in work-family conflict. In the present study, the score on work-family conflict (SWFC) among the employees is confined to less than 2.00, 2.00 to 3.00; 3.01 to 4.00 and above 4.00. The distribution of employees on the basis of their SWFC is given in Table 4.25.

Table 4.25: Score on WFC (SWFC) among the employees

Sl.No.	SWFC	Number of Employees in		Total
		PSBs	PRBs	
1.	Less than 2.00	62(20)	5(4.50)	67(15.91)
2.	2.00 - 3.00	103(33.23)	14(12.62)	117(27.79)
3.	3.01 - 4.00	113(36.45)	38(34.23)	151(35.87)
4.	Above 4.00	32(10.32)	54(48.65)	86(20.43)
	Total	**310(100)**	**111(100)**	**421(100)**

Note: Figures in brackets indicate percentage

The important SWFCs among the employees are 3.01 to 4.00 and 2.00 to 3.00 which constitute 35.87 and 27.79 per cent of their respective total. The employees with the SWFCs of above 4.00 constitute 20.43 per cent of the total. The important SWFCs among the employees in PSBs are 3.01 to 4.00 and 2.00 to 3.00 which constitute 36.45 and 33.23 per cent of their respective total. Among the employees in PRBs, these two are above 4.00 and 3.01 to 4.00 which constitute 48.65 and 34.23 per cent of their respective total.

The work-family conflict among the employees in PRBs is greater than that among the employees in PSBs.

Family-work Conflict among the Employees

Family-work conflict, also a form of inter-role conflict, is similar to work-family conflict. It occurs when "the role pressures from the family and work domains are mutually incompatiable in some respect" (Greenhays and Beutell, 1985); when the emphasis is on family and the conflict that transpires when family responsibilities conflict with an individual's work-related duties is family-work conflict. Family-work conflict is more apt to exert negative influences in the home domain, because more conflict in the family unit, and constitute less life and job satisfaction (Netemeyer *et al.* 1996). The family work conflict (FWC) among the employees has been measured with the help of many variables related to FWC (Eagle *et al.* 1997;[14] Cooke and Rousseau, 1985).[15] In the present study, the FWC has been measured with the help of eight statements related to FWC. The respondents are asked to rate these statements at five point scale according to the order of existence in the banks from highly agree to highly disagree. The assigned scores on these scales are from 5 to 1 respectively.

The FWC among the employees in PSBs and PRBs has been measured with the help of the mean scores of the statements in FWC. The 't' test has been administered to find out the significant difference among the two groups of employees regarding their FWC. The overall FWC among the employees in PSBs and PRBs has been measured by the mean score of the statements in FWC. The results are given in Table 4.26.

The highly viewed FWCs among the employees in PSBs are the 'stress caused by the children affect the performance in work' and 'strained family relationship leads to stress on work place' since their respective mean scores are 3.8198 and 3.7617. Among the employees in PRBs, these statements are 'strained family relationship leads to stress on work place' and 'family causes lack of concentration on work' since their respective mean scores are 3.9897 and 3.9617. Regarding the FWC, the significant differences among the two group of employees have been noticed in the cases of 'family responsibilities prevent effective performance in the job', 'preoccupied with family matters', 'time spent on my family affairs affects the time I have to spend on work' and 'family causes lack of concentration on my work' since their respective 't' statistics are significant at five per cent level.

Table 4.26: Mean score on FWC among the employees

Sl. No.	Statements in FWC	Mean Score among Employees in		't' statistics
		PSBs	PRBs	
1.	My family responsibilities prevent me from effectively performing my job	3.1452	3.8252	2.2496*
2.	Due to stress at home, I am often preoccupied with family matters at work	3.0244	3.9451	-2.4547*
3.	The time spent on my family affairs affects the time I have to spend on work	3.6612	3.9446	-2.8908*
4.	The time spent on my family causes lack of concentration on my work	3.0662	3.9617	-2.8084*
5.	Strained family relationship leads to stress on work place	3.7617	3.9897	-0.4547
6.	Helpless family life creates stress at work place also	3.5089	3.3962	-0.4626
7.	Stress caused by the children affects my performance in work	3.8198	3.5627	0.6324
8.	My supervisors and peers dislike my pre-occupation with my personal life while at work	3.2545	3.8684	-0.9114

* *Significant at five per cent level.*

Reliability and Validity of Statements in Family Work Conflict (FWC)

The scores of the statements related to the FWC have been included for the Confirmatory Factor Analysis to test the validity and reliability of the statements in FWC. The result of Confirmatory Factor Analysis is given in Table 4.27. (*See table on next page*)

The convergent validity of the construct namely FWC has been verified since the 't' statistics of standardized factor loadings are significant at five per cent level. Since the composite validity of the construct is greater than 0.5 and the average variance extracted of the construct is greater than 50.00 per cent, the content validity of the construct has been confirmed. The reliability co-efficient of the

Table 4.27: Reliability and validity of statements related to family work conflict (FWC)

Sl. No.	Statements in FWC	Standardized Factor Loading	't' statistics	Composite Reliability	Average Variance Extracted	Reliability Co-efficient
1.	My family responsibilities prevent me from effectively performing my job	0.6734	3.0124*	0.7344	54.57	0.6974
2.	Due to stress at home, I am often preoccupied with family matters at work	0.7266	3.5024*			
3.	The time spent on my family affairs affect the time I have to spend on work	0.7451	4.0173*			
4.	The time spent on my family causes lack of concentration on my work	0.7204	3.3066*			
5.	The strained family relationship leads to stress on work place	0.7919	4.8963*			
6.	Helpless family life creates stress at work place also	0.8244	5.5907*			
7.	Stress caused by the children affects my performance in work	0.7644	4.3329*			
8.	My supervisors and peers dislike my pre-occupation with my personal life while at work	0.7339	3.4966*			

* *Significant at five per cent level.*

construct indicates that the included eight statements in this FWC explain FWC to the extent of 69.74 per cent. Hence, all the eight statements have been included to measure the FWC in the present study.

Score of Family-work Conflict (SFWC) among the Employees

The score of family-work conflict among the employees has been derived by the mean scores of the variables in family-work conflict. In the present study, the SFWC is confined to less than 2.0; 2.00 to 3.00; 3.01 to 4.00 and above 4.00. The distribution of employees on the basis of their SFWC is given in Table 4.28.

Table 4.28: Score of family-work conflict (SFWC) among the employees

Sl.No.	SFWC	Number of Employees in		Total
		PSBs	PRBs	
1.	Less than 2.00	57(18.39)	12(10.81)	69(16.39)
2.	2.00 - 3.00	139(44.84)	12(10.81)	151(35.87)
3.	3.01 - 4.00	76(24.52)	56(50.45)	132(31.35)
4.	Above 4.00	38(12.26)	31(27.93)	69(16.39)
	Total	**310(100)**	**111(100)**	**421(100)**

Note: Figures in brackets indicate percentage

The important SFWC among the employees are 2.00 to 3.00 and 3.01 to 4.00 which constitute 35.87 and 31.35 per cent of their respective total. The employees with the SFWC of above 4.00 constitute 16.39 per cent of the total. The important SFWC among the employees in PSBs are 2.00 to 3.00 and 3.01 to 4.00 which constitute 44.84 and 24.52 per cent of their respective total. Among the employees in PRBs, these are 3.01 to 4.00 and above 4.00 which constitute 50.45 and 27.93 per cent of their respective total. The SFWC among the employees in PRBs is greater than among the employees in PSBs.

Association between Profile of Employees and their Work-life Imbalance

The association between the profile of employees and their work-life imbalance is examined in two dimensions namely work-family conflict and family-work conflict. The profile variables included in the present study are age, educational qualification, personal income and years of experience. The one-way analysis of variance has been executed to examine the association. The result of one way analysis variance is illustrated in Table 4.29.

Table 4.29: Association between profile variables of employees and their SWFC and SFWC

Sl.No.	Profile Variables	F-statistics in	
		SWFC	SFWC
1.	Age	3.9904*	2.9614*
2.	Educational qualification	2.9446*	2.8546*
3.	Personal Income	2.8334*	2.8783*
4.	Years of experience	2.8554*	3.0942*

* *Significant at five per cent level.*

Regarding the SWFC, the significantly associating profile variables are age, educational qualification, personal income and years of experience since their respective 'F' statistics are significant at five per cent level. The profile variables that significantly associate with the SFWC among the employees are age, educational qualification, personal income and years of experience since their respective 'F' statistics are significant at five per cent level. The analysis reveals that the control variables namely age, educational qualification, personal income and years of experience are significantly associated with their work-family conflict and family-work conflict.

Association between Family Domain Variables and SWFC and SFWC among the Employees

Since the family domain variables are highly associated with the SWFC and SFWC among the employees, the present study has made an attempt to analyse such association with the help of one way analysis of variance. The included family domain variables are marital status, type of family, family size, number of family members per family, level of education of spouse, employment of spouse, parental status, age of the youngest child, family income, caring responsibilities and time devoted to family work per day. The result of one way analysis of variance is given in Table 4.30.

Table 4.30: Association between family domain variables and SWFC and SFWC

Sl. No.	Family Domain Variables	F-statistics Regarding	
		SWFC	SFWC
1.	Marital Status	2.9334*	2.8189*
2.	Type of family	2.8142	2.0664
3.	Family size	1.1568	3.0434*
4.	Number of earning members per family	2.8644*	1.4681
5.	Level of education of spouse	3.6994*	2.2194
6.	Employment of spouse	3.9693*	1.7711
7.	Parental status	1.6933	1.3089
8.	Age of the youngest child	2.4598*	3.4407*
9.	Family Income	2.6697*	2.8724*
10.	Caring responsibilities	2.5689*	2.4347*
11.	Time devoted to family work per day	2.6292*	2.5592*

* *Significant at five per cent level.*

Regarding the SWFC, the significantly associating family domain variables are marital status, number of earning members per family, level of education of spouse, employment of spouse, age of the youngest child, family income, caring responsibilities and time devoted to family work per day since their respective 'F' statistics are significant at five per cent level. The significantly associating family domain variables regarding the SFWC, are marital status, family size, age of the youngest child, family income, caring responsibilities and time devoted to family work per day since their respective 'F' statistics are significant at five per cent level.

Association between Organization Variables and the SWFC and SFWC among the Employees

The association between the organization variables of the employees and their SWFC and SFWC has been examined with the help of one way analysis of variance. The included organization variables are designation, hours worked per day and working schedule. The results of one way analysis of variance are shown in Table 4.31.

Table 4.31: Association between organization variables among employees and their SWFC and SFWC

Sl.No.	Organization Variables	F-statistics Regarding	
		SWFC	SFWC
1.	Designation	2.3654	3.0214*
2.	Hours worked per day	3.0911*	2.7637*
3.	Working schedule	3.1144*	3.2663*

* *Significant at 5 per cent level.*

Regarding the SWFC, the significantly associating organization variables are hours worked per day and working schedule since their respective 'F' statistics are significant at five per cent level. Regarding the SFWC, the significant organization variables are designation, hours of work per day and working schedule since their respective 'F' statistics are significant at five per cent level. The anlaysis reveals the importance of the organization variables in Work-family conflict and Family-work conflict among the employees.

Relationship between the Work Domain Variables and the WFC and FWC among the Employees

Since work domain variables may be related to the WFC and FWC among the employees, the present study has made an attempt to analyse the relation ship between work domain variables and WFC and FWC with the help of correlation analysis. The included work domain variables are unsupportive colleagues, pressure on work, performance inhibitions, lack of empowerment, effort reward imbalance, working hours and working conditions. The scores of the above said variables and the WFC and FWC have been included for the analysis.

The correlation co-efficients are presented in Table 4.32.

Regarding the WFC, the significantly correlated work domain variables are unsupportive colleagues, pressure on work, effort reward imbalance and working hours since their respective correlation co-efficients are significant at five per cent level. The significant correlation between work domain variables and FWC has been identified in the case of pressure on work. Since its correlation co-

Table 4.32: Relationship between work domain variables and the WFC and FWC

Sl. No.	Work Domain Variables	Correlation Co-efficient with	
		WFC	FWC
1.	Unsupportive colleagues	0.5317*	0.1033
2.	Work Pressure	0.5229*	0.3445*
3.	Performance Inhibitions	0.1032	0.1762
4.	Lack of Empowerment	0.2142	0.1042
5.	Effort-reward Imbalance	0.3443*	0.1519
6.	Working Hours	0.5242*	0.1263
7.	Working conditions	0.1029	0.1144

* *Significant at five per cent level.*

-efficient is significant at five per cent level. In all cases, the correlation co-efficients are positive. It reveals that the increase in work domain variables result in both WFC and FWC through higher correlation between work domain variables and WFC has been noticed.

LINKAGE BETWEEN ANTECEDENTS OF WORK-LIFE BALANCE AND WORK-LIFE BALANCE

Family and work are the two most important domains of life for most adults (Andrews and Withey, 1976).[16] When conflicts between these two domains occur, there are many adverse consequences on both individuals and organizations. Traditionally, researchers have viewed work-family conflict as a uni-directional construct. Recently, the bi-directional nature of work-family conflict has been recongnised by many researchers (Duxbury *et al.* 1992;[17] Gutek *et al.* 1991).[18] Carmen and Margaret (2001) developed two models of the determinants of work-family conflict. These two models are depicted in Figure 4.1. (*See fig. on next page*)

The model – A shows the determinants of family work conflict.

The model – B indicates the determinants of work-family conflict. Based on the above-said models, the present study analyses the linkage between the determinants of FWC and WFC among the employees.

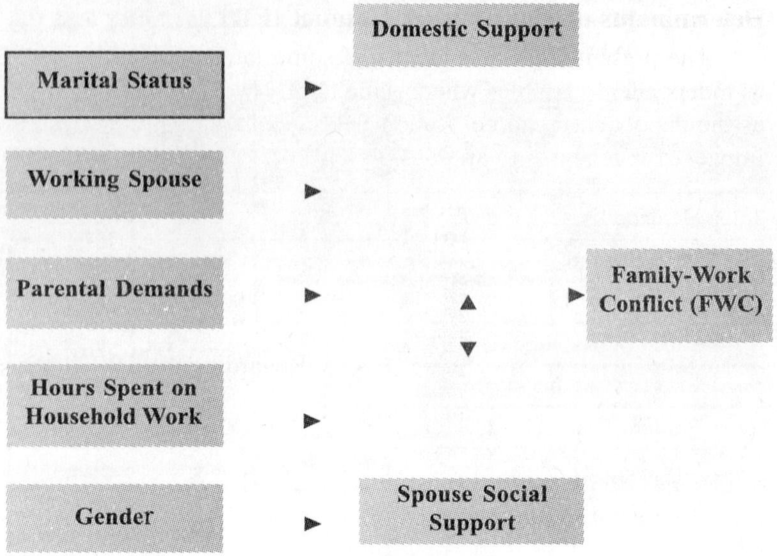

Domestic Support

Marital Status

Working Spouse

Parental Demands

Family-Work Conflict (FWC)

Hours Spent on Household Work

Gender

Spouse Social Support

Fig. 4.1: Model – A

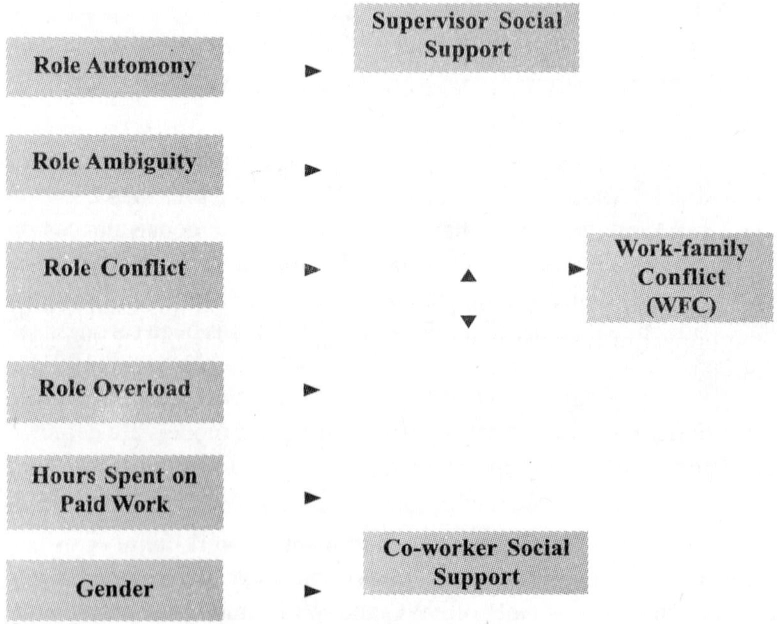

Supervisor Social Support

Role Automony

Role Ambiguity

Role Conflict

Work-family Conflict (WFC)

Role Overload

Hours Spent on Paid Work

Gender

Co-worker Social Support

Fig. 4.2: Model – B

Determinants of Family-work Conflict (FWC)

The present study has identified some family related variables as independent variables whereas the family-work conflict is treated as the dependent variable. A model has been created to analyse the impact of independent variables on FWC. It is given in Figure 4.3.

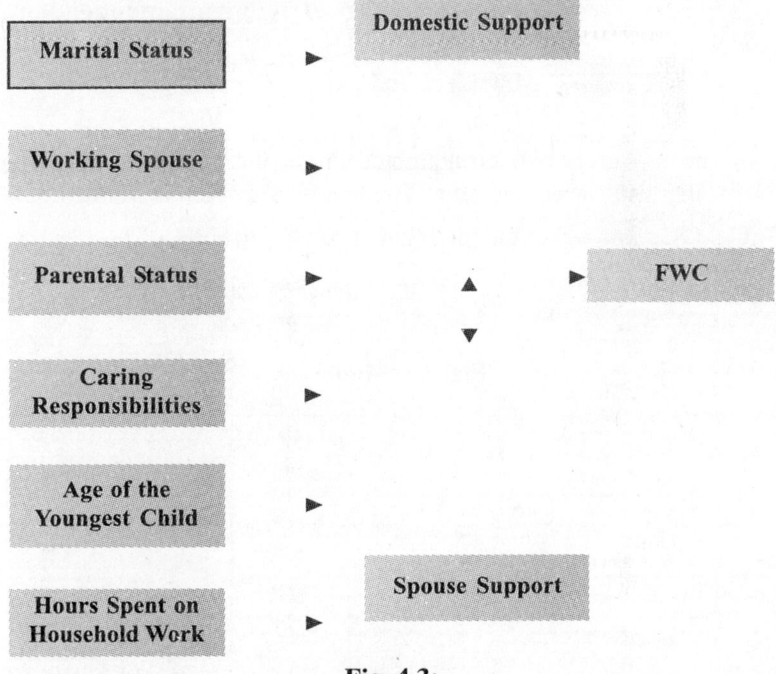

Fig. 4.3:

The multiple regression analysis has been administered to prove the impact of independent variables on FWC. The fitted regression model is

$$Y = a+b_1x_1+b_2x_2+b_3x_3+b_4x_4+b_5x_5+b_6x_6+b_7x_7+b_8x_8+e$$

Where

Y – Score on FWC

x_1 – Marital Status of the employees

x_2 – Working Spouse

x_3 – Parental Status

x_4 – Caring responsibilities

x_5 – Age of the youngest child

x_6 – Hours spent on household work

x_7 – Score on Domestic Support

x_8 – Score on spouse support

$b_1, b_2 \ldots b_6$ – Regression co-efficient of independent variables

a – Intercept and

e – Error term.

The impacts have been examined among the employees in PSBs, PRBs and also for pooled data. The results are given in Table 4.33.

Table 4.33: Impact of independent variables on FWC

Sl. No.	Independent Variables	Regression Co-efficient among Employees in		
		PSBs	PRBs	Pooled
1.	Marital Status	0.0485	0.2408*	0.1382*
2.	Working Spouse	0.2142*	0.2962*	0.2526*
3.	Parental Status	0.1334*	0.1084	0.1021
4.	Caring responsibilities	0.1089	0.1661*	0.1469*
5.	Age of the youngest child	-0.1408*	0.0893	0.0884
6.	Hours spent on household work	0.3029*	0.2802*	0.2917*
7.	Domestic support	-0.2965*	-0.3145*	-0.2245*
8.	Spouse support	-0.3442*	-0.2601*	-0.2808*
	Constant	0.4586	0.9193	0.8246
	R^2	0.8483	0.7868	0.8814
	F-statistics	11.9697*	9.4523*	13.0969*

** Significant at five per cent level.*

In the PSBs, the significantly influencing variables on the family-work conflict among the employees are working spouse, parental status, age of the youngest child, hours spent on household work, domestic support and spouse support since their regression co-efficients are significant at five per cent level. A unit increase in the level of spouse support, domestic support and age of the youngest child, would result in a decline in FWC among the employees by 0.3442, 0.2965 and 0.1408 units respectively. A unit increase in hours spent on household work, parental status, working spouse, would result in an increase in FWC by 0.3029, 0.1334 and 0.2142 units respectively. The change in independent variables explains the changes in FWC among the employees in PSBs to the extent of 84.83 per cent.

The significantly influencing independent variables on the FWC among the employees in PRBs are marital status, working spouse, caring responsibilities, hours spent on household work, domestic support and spouse support. A unit increase in the marital status, working spouse, caring responsibilities and hours spent on household work would result in an increase in FWC by 0.2408, 0.2962, 0.1661 and 0.2802 units respectively. A unit increase in domestic and spouse support would result in a decrease in FWC by 0.3145 and 0.2601 units respectively. The changes in the independent variables explain the changes in FWC to the extent of 78.68 per cent since its co-efficient of determination is 0.7868. The analysis reveals that the domestic and spouse supports reduce the FWC to a considerable extent whereas the working spouse and hours spent on house work increase the FWC among the bank employees.

Determinants of Work-family Conflict (WFC)

The two important determinants of WFC are work domain variables and organizational role stressors. Apart from this, the supervisor and co-worker supports also have their own influence on the WFC. Hence the present study has made an attempt to analyse the impact of work domain variables and social support on WFC initially.

1. Impact of Work Domain Variables and Social Support on Work-Family Conflict (WFC)

It is imperative to analyse the impact of work domain variables on work-family conflict among the employees for some policy implications. The impact has been measured among the employees in PSBs, PRBs and also for pooled data separately. The multiple regression analysis has been administered to analyse the impact. The fitted regression model is

$$Y = a + b_1x_1 + b_2x_2 + b_3x_3 + b_4x_4 + b_5x_5 + b_6x_6 + b_7x_7 + e$$

Where

y = WFC among the employees
X_1 = Score on unsupportive colleagues
X_2 = Score on pressure on work
X_3 = Score on performance inhibition
X_4 = Score on lack of empowerment
X_5 = Score on effort-reward imbalance
X_6 = Score on working hours
X_7 = Score on working conditions
X_8 = Score on supervisor's support
X_9 = Score on co-worker's support
$B_1, b_2, \ldots b_7$ = Regression co-efficient of independent variables
a = Intercept and
b = Error term

The result of regression analysis is given in Table 4.34.

Table 4.34: Impact of work domain variables and social support on WFC

Sl. No.	Work Domain Variables	Regression Co-efficient among Employees in		
		PSBs	PRBs	Pooled
1.	Unsupportive colleagues	0.3914*	0.4503*	0.4209*
2.	Work Pressure	0.1802*	0.4114*	0.2863*
3.	Performance inhibitors	0.0962	0.1231	0.1017
4.	Lack of empowerment	0.1123	0.1886*	0.1445*
5.	Effort reward imbalance	0.0565	0.0969	0.0661
6.	Working hours	0.2451*	0.4635*	0.3806*
7.	Working conditions	0.063	0.1023	0.0962
8.	supervisor's support	-0.3145*	-0.2908*	-0.2911*
9.	Co-workers' support	-0.2021*	-0.3086*	-0.2546*
	Constant	0.8962	1.3561	1.6516
	R^2	0.8144	0.8909	0.9303
	F-statistics	11.0896*	14.3083*	15.4145*

* *Significant at five per cent level.*

The significantly influencing working domain variables on WFC among the employees in PSBs are unsupportive colleagues, work pressure and working hours. A unit increase in the perception on the above said work domain variables would result in an increase in WFC by 0.3914, 0.1802 and 0.2451 units respectively. Among the employees in PRBs, a unit increase on the perception on unsupportive colleagues, pressure on work, lack of empowerment and working hours would result in an increase in WFC by 0.4503, 0.4114, 0.1886 and 0.4635 units respectively. The analysis of pooled data reveals the significant impact of unsupportive colleagues, pressure on work, lack of empowerment and working hours. The analysis in the perception of work domain variables explains the changes in WFC to the extent of 93.03 per cent. The analysis reveals the importance of working hours and unsupportive colleagues in the determination of WFC among the employees. The negative impact of work domain variables on the WFC among the employees is comparatively higher among the employees in PRBs than in PSBs.

The social support of the employees has a significant negative impact on WFC among the employees in PSBs and PRBs since their regression co-efficients are significant at five per cent level. In the case of PSBs, a unit, increase in the supervisor's support and co-workers' support would reduce the WFC by 0.3145 and 0.2021 units respectively. In the case of PRBs, these two supports reduce the WFC by 0.2908 and 0.3086 units respectively.

2. *Impact of Role Stressors and Social Support on WFC*

The organizational role stress may have its own impact on the work-family conflict. Hence the present study has made an attempt to analyse the impact of role stressors and social supports on WFC for some policy implications. The multiple regression analysis has been executed to analyse such impact. The fitted regression model is

$$Y = a+b_1x_1+b_2x_2+b_3x_3+b_4x_4+b_5x_5+b_6x_6+e$$

Where

Y – WFC among the employees

X_1 – Lack of role autonomy among the employees

X_2 – Role ambiguity among the employees

X_3 – Role conflict among the employees

X_4 – Role overload among the employees
X_5 – Score on supervisor support
X_6 – Score on co-worker support
$b_1, b_2, \ldots b_6$ – Regression co-efficient of independent variables
a – Intercept and
e – Error term

The impact of role stressors and social support on WFC among the employees in PSBs, PRBs and also for pooled data has been measured separately. The results are given in Table 4.35.

Table 4.35: Impact of organizational role stress and social support on WFC

Sl. No.	Independent Variables	Regression Co-efficient among Employees in		
		PSBs	PRBs	Pooled
1.	Lack of role autonomy	0.0966	0.1917*	0.1643*
2.	Role ambiguity	0.2103*	0.0844	0.0845
3.	Role conflict	0.1808*	0.1447*	0.1408*
4.	Role overload	0.1847*	0.2865*	0.2109*
5.	Supervisor's support	-0.1896*	-0.2703*	-0.1929*
6.	Co-workers' support	-0.2144*	-0.2714*	-0.2204*
	Constant	0.8917	1.3446	1.0462
	R^2	0.8142	0.7081	0.8459
	F-statistics	9.8408*	7.3042*	10.1476*

** Significant at five per cent level.*

The significantly influencing role stressors are role ambiguity, role conflict and role overload among the employees in PSBs since their respective regression co-efficients are significant at five per cent level. A unit increase in the above said three variables would result in an increase in WFC by 0.2103, 0.1808 and 0.1847 units respectively. At the same time, a unit increase in the supervisor and co-worker support would result in a significant decrease of WFC by 0.1896 and 0.2144 units respectively.

In the case of PRBs, a unit increase in lack of role autonomy, role conflict and role over load would result in an increase in WFC by 0.1917, 0.1447 and 0.2865 units respectively. A unit increase in the supervisor and co-worker support would result in a decrease in WFC by 0.2703 and 0.2714 units respectively. The analysis of pooled data reveals the significant impact of lack of role autonomy, role conflict, roles overload, supervisor and co-worker support on the WFC. The changes in independent variables explain the changes in WFC to the extent of 84.59 per cent.

References

1. Zedeck, S. (1992), *Introduction: Exploring the Domain of Work and Family Concerns*. In S. Zedeck, (Ed), Work, Families, and Organizations, San Francisco: Jossey-Bass".
2. Thomas, L.T. and Hauster, D.C. (1995), "Impact of family-support Work Variables on Work-family Conflict and Strain: A Control Perspective", *Journal of Applied Psychology*, 80(4): 6-15.
3. Duxlury, L.E., and Higgins, C.A. (1991), "Gender Differences in Work-family Conflict," *Journal of Applied Psychology*, 76(2): 60-74.
4. Frone, M.R., Yardly, J.K., and Marhel, K.S. (1997), "Developing and Testing An Integrative Model of the Work-family Interface", *Journal of Vocational Behaviour*, 50(1): 36-47.
5 Frone, M.R., and Yardely, J.K. (1996), "Work Place Family Supportive Programmes: *Predictors and Organizational Psychology*", 69(4): 351-366.
6. Kopelman, R.E., Greenhaus, J.H. and Connolly, T.R. (1983), "A Model of Work, Family and Inter Role Conflict – A Construct Validation Study", *Organizational Behaviour and Human Performance*, 32(3): 198-215.
7. Gutek, B.A., Searle, S and Klepa, L. (1991), "Rational *vs.* Gender Role Explanations for Work-family Conflict", *Journal of Applied Psychology,* 76(4): 560-568.
8. Kahn, R.L., Wolfe, D., Quinn, R., Snoek, J. and Rosenthal, R. (1964), *Organizational Stress: Studies in the Role Conflict and Role Ambiguity*, John Waley, New York, NY.
9. Pareek, V. (1983), *Role Stress Scale: ORS Scale Booklet, Answer Sheet and Manual*, Navin Publications, Ahmedabad.
10. Pareek, U. (1997), *Training Instruments for Human Resource Development*, Tata McGraw Hill, New Delhi.
11. Greenhaus, J.H., and Beutell, N.J. (1985), "Sources of Conflict between Work and Family Roles", *Academy of Management Review*, 10(1): 76-88.

12. Carlson, D.S., Kacman, K,M., and Williams, L.J. (2000), "Construct and Initial Validation of A Multidimensional Measure of Work-family Conflict", *Journal of Vocational Behaviur*, 56(2): 249-276.
13. Frone, M.R., Russel, M., and Barnes, G.M. (1996), "Work-family Conflict, Gender, and Health Related Outcomes: A Study of Employed Parents in Two Community Samples", *Journal of Occupational Health Psychology*, 1(1): 57-69.
14. Eagle, B., Miles, E. and Icenogle, M. (1997), "Interrde Conflicts and Permeability of Work and Family Domains: Are these Gender Differences?", *Journal of Vocational Behaviour,* 50: 168-184.
15. Cooke, R and Rousseau, D. (1985), "Stress and Strain from Family Roles and Work-role Expectations", *Journal of Applied Psychology*, 69(2): 252-260.
16. Andrews, F., and Withey, S. (1976), *Social Indicators*, Plenum Press, New York.
17. Duxbury, L.E., and Higgions, C.A. (1992), "Gender Differences in Work-family Conflict", *Journal of Applied Psychology,* 76(1): 60-74.
18. Gutek, B.A., Searle, S. and Klepa, L. (1991), "Rational *vs.* Gender Role Explanations for Work-family Conflict", *Journal of Applied Psychology,* 76(4): 560-568.

5

Consequences of Work-life Imbalance

INTRODUCTION

The consequences of work-family conflicts and family-work conflicts have a number of negative outcomes. Work and family conflicts have been identified as sources of psychological strain among married men and women (Frone *et al.,* 1992);[1] work and family conflicts have been found to lead to decrements in psychological and physical well-being of employees (Bedeian *et al.,* 1988;[2] Burden and Goozins, 1987).[3] The relationship between work-family conflict with life satisfaction is a negative one (Aryee, 1992;[4] Judge *et al.,* 1994).[5] Bedeian *et al.* (1988) argued that when work interferes with family life, this conflict is often released on the family, causing poor marital adjustment which ends with lower levels of life satisfaction. The work-family conflict has a significant relationship with family domain outcomes (Higgins *et al.,* 1992).[6]

The work-family interface may have its own influence on the outcomes related to the organization, employee and the family. The intrinsic motivation among the employees may be affected by the negative work-family interface. Whether it may be work-family conflict or family-work conflict, it creates the consequences on various aspects and finally job performance. The initial outcome is the 'Emotional Exhaustion'. It refers to 'a form of interole conflict in which the general demands of time devoted to, and strain created by the job interface, with performing family-related responsibilities (Boles *et al.,* 1997).[7] The emotional exhaustion may influence on the organization commitment, job satisfaction, job stress, intention to turnover, overall rating of organization and absenteeism among the employees (Low *et al.,* 2001;[8] Keaveney, 1992;[9] Miller, 2002;[10] Allen *et al.,* 2000)[11] which are related to the organizational outcome.

Thomas and Gauster (1995)[12] suggested that parental demands may interfere with daily job activities and occupational achievement. The family-work conflict is generally associated with negative work domain outcomes such as work-related withdrawals or absenteeism (Goff *et al.,* 1990).[13] Mac Ewen and Barling (1994)[14] found that family-work conflict was positively related to work withdrawal. In the present study, the outcomes of the work-family interface (WFC and FWC) have been discussed at four different dimensions namely organization outcome, family outcome, employment outcome and finally job performance. The organizational outcome of the work-family interface has been analyzed initially.

ORGANIZATIONAL COMMITMENT AMONG THE EMPLOYEES

Organizational commitment is defined as "the relative strength of an individual's identification with and involvement in a particular organization" (Steers, 1977). The organizational commitment, among the employees, has been measured with the help of seven statements related to organizational commitment. The employees are asked to rate the given seven statements at five point scale according to their level of perception at their organization from highly agree to highly disagree. The assigned scores on these scales are from 5 to 1 respectively.

The level of organizational commitment among the employees has been examined with the help of the mean scores of the statements related to organizational commitment. The mean scores of the statements among the employees in PSBs and PRBs have been computed separately in order to exhibit the level of organizational commitment among them. Regarding the organizational commitment, the significant differences among the two groups of employees have been analysed with the help of *'t'* test. The results are presented in Table 5.1.

Table 5.1: Mean score on organizational commitment among the employees

Sl. No.	Statements in Organizational Commitment	Mean Scores among Employees in		't' statistics
		PSBS	PRBs	
1.	I would be happy to spend the rest of my career with this bank	3.8673	2.9196	2.4543*
2.	I enjoy discussing the bank with outsiders	3.2455	2.4541	2.1717*
3.	I feel as if this bank's problems are my own	3.3045	2.3132	2.8589*
4.	I feel as if I am like a part of the bank	3.5096	2.6065	2.4196*
5.	I feel emotionally attached to the bank	3.6161	2.5091	2.9692*
6.	The bank means a lot to me personally	3.6144	2.4561	2.0841*
7.	I have a strong sense of belonging to the bank	3.4542	2.3962	3.1492*

**Significant at five per cent level.*

The highly viewed statements in organizational commitment among the employees in PSBs are 'spend the rest of my career in the bank' and 'emotionally attached to the bank' since their respective mean scores are 3.8673 and 3.6161. Among the employees in PRBs, these two are 'spend the rest of my career in the bank' and 'proud to be part of the bank' since their mean scores are 2.9196 and 2.6065 respectively. Regarding the organizational commitment, the significant differences among the two groups of employees have been identified in all the seven statements since their respective *'t'* statistics are significant at five per cent level.

Reliability and Validity of Statements in Organizational Commitment

The reliability and validity of the statements in organizational commitment have been examined with the help of Confirmatory Factor Analysis (CFA). The scores of the variables in organizational commitment have been used for the analysis. The result of CFA is given in Table 5.2.

Table 5.2: Reliability and validity of statements in organizational commitment

Sl. No.	Statements	Standardized Factor Loading	't' statistics	Composite Reliability	Average Variance Extracted	Reliability
1.	I would be happy to spend the rest of my career with this bank	0.7501	2.4082*	0.7144	52.49	0.7316
2.	I enjoy discussing the bank with outsiders	0.7819	2.7914*			
3.	I feel as if this bank's problems are my own	0.8244	3.6048*			
4.	I feel as if I am like a part of the bank	0.7711	2.6621*			
5.	I feel emotionally attached to the bank	0.7236	2.3346*			
6.	The bank means a lot to me personally	0.8519	3.9941*			
7.	I have a strong sense of belonging to the bank	0.8011	3.1445*			

* *Significant at five per cent level.*

Table 5.2 reveals the standardized factor loading and '*t*' statistics of the statements related to organizational commitment. The composite reliability, average variance extracted and reliability co-efficient of the organizational commitment are also presented in the table. Since the '*t*' statistics of the standardized factor loading of the statements in the organizational commitment are significant at five per cent level, its convergent validity has been confirmed. The composite reliability co-efficient is greater than the minimum threshold of 0.5. The average variance extracted by the construct is greater than 50 per cent which confirms the convergent validity of the construct, namely organizational commitment. The reliability co-efficient of the construct indicates that the included seven statements in the construct, explain the organizational commitment to the extent of 73.16 per cent. Hence, all the seven statements have been included to analyse the organizational commitment among the employees.

Score on Organizational Commitment (SOC) among the Employees

The scores on organizational commitment among the employees have been computed by the mean score of the variables included in organizational commitment. The SOC among the employees is confined to less than 2.00; 2.00 to 3.00; 3.01 to 4.00 and above 4.00. The distribution of employees on the basis of their SOC is given in Table 5.3.

Table 5.3: Score on organizational commitment (SOC) among the employees

Sl.No.	SOC	Number of Employees in		Total
		PSBs	PRBs	
1.	Less than 2.00	58(18.71)	32(28.83)	90(21.38)
2.	2.00 - 3.00	83(26.77)	39(35.14)	122(28.98)
3.	3.01 - 4.00	98(31.61)	24(21.62)	122(28.98)
4.	Above 4.00	71(22.91)	16(14.41)	87(20.66)
	Total	**310(100)**	**111(100)**	**421(100)**

Note: Figures in brackets indicate percentage

The important SOC among the employees are 3.01 to 4.00 and 2.00 to 3.00 which constitute 28.98 per cent of their respective total. The employees with the SOC of above 4.00 constitute 20.67 per cent of the total. The important SOC among the employees in PSBs are 3.01 to 4.00 and 2.00 to 3.00 which constitute 31.61 and 26.77 per cent of their respective total. Among the employees in PRBs, these two are 2.00 to 3.00 and less than 2.00 which constitute 35.14 and 28.83 per cent of their respective total. The analysis reveals that the SOC among the employees in PSBs is higher than that among the employees in PRBs.

JOB SATISFACTION AMONG EMPLOYEES

Job satisfaction is one of the important organizational outcomes. The job satisfaction scale includes a general job satisfaction item and Mc Donald and Mac Intyres (1997)[15] previously validated a ten-item scale with the reliability co-efficient of 0.80. In the present study, the job satisfaction among the employees has been examined with the help of 12 related variables. The employees are asked to rate the 12 variables at five point scale from highly satisfied to highly dissatisfied. The assigned marks on these scales are from 5 to 1 respectively.

The level of job satisfaction among the employees has been examined with the mean scores of the variables in job satisfaction among the employees in PSBs and PRBs separately. Regarding the level of job satisfaction, the significant differences among the two groups of employees have been analysed with the help of '*t*' test. The overall job satisfaction among the employees has been derived from the mean scores of the 12 variables included in job satisfaction. The results are given in Table 5.4.

Table 5.4: Mean score of variables in job satisfaction among the employees

Sl. No.	Variables in Job Satisfaction	Mean Scores among Employees in		't' statistics
		PSBs	PRBs	
1.	Nature of work	3.6514	2.8417	2.1409*
2.	Organizational supervisor	3.4502	2.5096	2.9663*
3.	Relationship with co-workers	3.5778	2.6142	2.7803*
4.	Pay	3.8189	3.0183	2.6814*
5.	Fringe benefits	3.9226	3.2662	2.2963*
6.	Scope for promotion or advancement	2.9697	2.8617	0.3914
7.	Job Situation	3.0139	2.8969	0.4217
8.	Work load	3.2685	2.1718	2.8969*
9.	Job security	3.8664	2.2104	3.7334*
10.	Training and development opportunities	3.8143	3.0926	2.1445*
11.	Sorts of things they do	3.7791	2.6166	3.0969*
12.	Ability to meet career goals	3.6169	2.8082	3.1414*

* *Significant at five per cent level.*

The highly satisfied variables among the employees in PSBs are 'fringe benefits', 'job security', 'pay' and 'training and development opportunities' since their mean scores are 3.9226, 3.8665, 3.8189 and 3.8143 respectively. Among the employees in PRBs, these variables are 'fringe benefits', 'training and development opportunities' and 'pay' since their mean scores are 3.2662, 3.0926 and 3.0183 respectively. Regarding the level of job satisfaction, the significant differences among the employees in PSBs and PRBs have been noticed in the case of 'nature of work', 'organizational supervisor', 'relationship with co-workers', 'pay', 'fringe benefits', 'work load', 'job security', 'training and development opportunities', 'sorts of things they do' and 'ability to meet career goals' since their respective '*t*' statistics are significant at five per cent level.

Reliability and Validity of Variables in Job Satisfaction

Totally, there are 12 variables included to measure job satisfaction. Before summarizing the level of job satisfaction, it is imperative to test the reliability and validity of variables in job satisfaction. Hence the present study has executed the CFA. The result of CFA is given in Table 5.5.

Table 5.5: Reliability and validity of variables of job satisfaction

Sl. No.	Variable in Job Satisfaction	Standardized Factor Loading	'*t*' statistics	Composite Reliability	Average Variance Extracted	Reliability
1.	Nature of work	0.6973	3.1574*	6.7568	52.41	0.6917
2.	Organizational supervisor	0.7392	3.5443*			
3.	Relationship with co-workers	0.7669	3.7742*			
4.	Pay	0.8644	5.0331*			
5.	Fringe benefits	0.8243	5.5617*			
6.	Scope for promotion or advancement	0.7568	3.6241*			
7.	Job situation	0.6884	3.1247*			
8.	Work load	0.7331	3.4092*			
9.	Job security	0.7869	3.9193*			
10.	Training and development opportunities	0.6773	3.0994*			
11.	Sorts of things they do	0.7445	3.6907*			
12.	Ability to meet career goals	0.6569	3.0751*			

* *Significant at five per cent level.*

The standardized factor loading of the variables in job satisfaction varies from 0.6569 to 0.8644. All standardized factor loadings are significant at five per cent level. It reveals the convergent validity of the variables to the construct. The composite validity of the construct is greater than 0.5. It also confirms the convergent validity of the construct. The average variance extracted by the construct is greater than the minimum threshold of 50 per cent. The reliability co-efficient of the construct reveals that the included twelve variables in job satisfaction explain it to the extent of 69.17 per cent. Since the variables included in job satisfaction satisfy the reliability and validity of the construct, these twelve variables have been included for estimating the job satisfaction among the employees.

Score on Level of Job Satisfaction among the Employees (SLJS)

The level of job satisfaction among the employees has been computed by the mean scores of the variables in job satisfaction. The SLJS in the present study is confined to less than 2.00; 2.00 to 3.00; 3.01 to 4.00 and above 4.00. The distribution of employees on the basis of their SLJS is given in Table 5.6.

Table 5.6: Score on level of job satisfaction (SLJS) among the employees

Sl.No.	SLJS	Number of Employees in		Total
		PSBs	PRBs	
1.	Less than 2.00	67(21.61)	29(26.13)	96(22.80)
2.	2.00 - 3.00	88(28.39)	47(42.34)	135(32.07)
3.	3.01 - 4.00	103(33.23)	24(21.62)	127(30.17)
4.	Above 4.00	52(16.77)	11(9.91)	63(14.96)
	Total	**310(100)**	**111(100)**	**421(100)**

Note: Figures in brackets indicate percentage

The important SLJS among the employees are 2.00 to 3.00 and 3.01 to 4.00 which constitute 32.07 and 30.17 per cent of their respective total. The employees with the SLJS of above 4.00 constitute 14.96 per cent of the total. The important SLJS among the employees in PSBs are 3.01 to 4.00 and 2.00 to 3.00 which constitute 33.23 and 28.39 per cent of their respective total. Among the employees in PRBs, these two are 2.00 to 3.00 and less than 2.00 which constitute

42.34 and 26.13 per cent of their respective total. The analysis reveals that there is a higher level of job satisfaction among the employees in PSBs than in PRBs.

JOB STRESS AMONG THE EMPLOYEES

Job stress is one of the important outcomes of the work-family conflict and family-work conflict (Chandraiah *et al*., 2003).[16] The Job Stress Inventory (JSI) was developed to provide a tool to measure relative levels of sources of stress in the work place. The JSI is empirically based, normed, and lends itself to a variety of work place applications (Beehr and Newman, 1978).[17] The JSI was constructed to measure both generic and specific stressors, and in particular, work-related areas. The JSI measures nine sources of occupational stress, namely physical demands and danger, uncertainty, lack of inter-personal skills of others, time pressure, lack of competence of supervisor, lack of competence of others, lack of control and red tape (Parik *et al*., 2004;[18] Henle and Anita, 2008).[19] In the present study, the job stress among the employees has been measured with the help of eighteen measures. The employees are asked to rate the work stress variables in their organization at five point scale from very high to very low. The marks assigned on these scales are from 5 to 1 respectively.

The level of job stress among the employees has been computed from the mean scores of the variables in job stress. Regarding the job stress variables, the significant differences among the employees in PSBs and PRBs have been examined with the help of '*t*' test. The results are explained in Table 5.7.

Table 5.7: Mean scores of job stress variables among the employees

Sl. No.	Job Stress Variables	Mean Scores among Employees in		'*t*' statistics
		PSBs	PRBs	
1	2	3		4
1.	Work load	3.2141	4.1869	-3.2449*
2.	Complexity of work	3.3399	3.8646	-1.9965*
3.	Poor leadership	2.4586	3.3961	-2.8129*
4.	Poor working conditions	2.3144	2.2566	0.2696

Contd...

1	2	3		4
5.	Low pay	2.4108	2.7182	-0.5968
6.	Monotony of work	3.1144	3.9697	-2.9334*
7.	Poor career prospects	2.8684	3.8641	-2.9619*
8.	Work posture	3.0417	3.9197	-3.6244*
9.	Discrimination	2.4085	3.7667	-3.4916*
10.	Low social support	2.6675	3.8224	-3.6872*
11.	Job insecurity	3.0514	4.3342	-3.0914*
12.	Too much responsibility	3.2869	4.1145	-2.1496*
13.	Low participation in decision-making	2.1543	3.8569	-4.2261*
14.	Less liberties	3.1411	4.2565	-2.2491*
15.	Conflicting demands	2.8644	3.8144	-2.8824*
16.	Unstandardised pay structure	2.5106	3.4497	-2.7339*
17.	Absence of human orientation	2.3088	3.2518	-2.9196*
18.	Flexible labour contract	2.5197	3.4517	-3.0841*

** Significant at five per cent level.*

The highly stressed variables among the employees in PSBs are 'complexity of work', 'too much responsibility' and 'work load' since their respective mean scores are 3.3399, 3.2869 and 3.2141. Among the employees in PRBs the highly stressed variables are 'job insecurity', 'less liberties' and 'work load' since their respective mean scores are 4.3342, 4.2565 and 4.1869. Regarding the job stress variables, the significant differences among the two groups of employees have been noticed in the case of 'work load', 'complexity of work', 'poor leadership', 'monotony of work', 'poor career prospects', 'work posture', 'discrimination', 'low social support', 'job insecurity', 'too much responsibility', 'low participation in decision-making', 'less liberties', 'conflicting demands', 'unstandardised pay structure', 'absence of human orientation' and 'flexible labour contract' since their respective *'t'* statistics are significant at 5 per cent level.

Reliability and Validity of Variables in Job Stress

The score on the work stress variables has been included for confirmatory factor analysis in order to test the reliability and validity of the variables in job stress. The results are presented in Table 5.8.

Table 5.8: Reliability and validity of variables in job stress among the employees

Sl. No.	Variable in Job Stress	Standardized Factor Loading	't' statistics	Composite Reliability	Average Variance Extracted	Reliability
1.	Work load	0.8234	4.3963*	0.7456	53.71	0.7276
2.	Complexity of work	0.7667	3.1045*			
3.	Poor leadership	0.7244	2.8965*			
4.	Poor working conditions	0.6986	2.2948*			
5.	Low pay	0.8491	4.5596*			
6.	Monotony of work	0.7336	2.9147*			
7.	Poor career prospects	0.8087	4.1099*			
8.	Work posture	0.7552	3.5149*			
9.	Discrimination	0.6787	2.6996*			
10.	Low social support	0.6964	2.5913*			
11.	Job insecurity	0.7411	3.6617*			
12.	Too much responsibility	0.8246	4.4971*			
13.	Low participation in decision-making	0.7639	3.3653*			
14.	Less liberties	0.6845	3.6012*			
15.	Conflicting demands	0.7337	3.7177*			
16.	Unstandardised pay structure	0.8233	4.2865*			
17.	Absence of human orientation	0.6967	3.4266*			
18.	Flexible labour contract	0.7454	3.8062*			

* *Significant at five per cent level.*

The '*t*' statistics of the standard factor loading of the variables, related to job stress, are significant at five per cent level. The composite reliability is greater than the minimum threshold of 0.5. Both the two results confirm the convergent validity of the construct. The average variance extracted by the construct is greater than the standard minimum threshold of 50 per cent, which confirms the convergent validity. The reliability co-efficient of the construct reveals that the included 18 variables explain the job stress to the extent of 72.76 per cent. Hence, these 18 variables have been included to estimate the job stress among the employees in PSBs and PRBs.

Score on Level of Job Stress (LJS) among the Employees

The level of job stress among the employees is computed by the mean scores of the variables included in job stress. The LJS in the present study is confined to less than 2.00, 2.00 to 3.00; 3.01 to 4.00 and above 4.00. The distribution of employees on the basis of their level of job stress is given in Table 5.9.

Table 5.9: Score on level of job stress (LJS) among the employees

Sl.No.	LJS	Number of Employees in		Total
		PSBs	PRBs	
1.	Less than 2.00	59(19.03)	11(9.91)	70(16.64)
2.	2.00 - 3.00	153(49.35)	23(20.72)	176(41.81)
3.	3.01 - 4.00	62(20)	48(43.24)	110(26.13)
4.	Above 4.00	36(11.62)	29(26.13)	65(15.44)
	Total	**310(100)**	**111(100)**	**421(100)**

Note: Figures in brackets indicate percentage

The important levels of job stress among the employees are 2.00 to 3.00 and 3.01 to 4.00 which constitute 41.81 and 26.13 per cent of their respective total. The employees with the LJS of above 4.00 constitute 15.44 per cent of the total. The important LJS among the employees in PSBs are 2.00 to 3.00 and 3.01 to 4.00 which constitute 49.35 and 20.00 per cent of their respective total. Among the employees in PRBs these are 3.01 to 4.00 and above 4.00 which constitute 43.24 and 26.13 per cent of their respective total. The analysis infers that the level of job stress among the employees in PRBs is greater than among employees in PSBs.

ABSENTEEISM AMONG THE EMPLOYEES

The absenteeism among the employees is one of the outcomes of the work-life imbalance among them. The absenteeism leads to less productivity and poor interpersonal relationship among the employees. The causes for absenteeism may be too many, but the present study is confined to only six variables. The employees are asked to rate the above said six variables, related to absenteeism ,at five point scale according to the order of importance from highly agree to highly disagree. The assigned scores on these scales are from 5 to 1 respectively.

The level of absenteeism among the employees has been examined with the help of the mean scores of the variables related to absenteeism. The mean scores of the variables in absenteeism, among the employees in PSBs and PRBs, have been computed separately to exhibit the level of absenteeism among the employees. Regarding absenteeism, the significant difference among the employees in PSBs and PRBs have been examined with the help of *'t'* test. The results are presented in Table 5.10.

Table 5.10: Mean score of absenteeism among the employees

Sl. No.	Variables in Absenteeism	Mean Scores among Employees in		't' statistics
		PSBs	PRBs	
1.	Absenteeism due to ill-health	2.8186	3.8587	-3.8184*
2.	Absenteeism due to family-related problems	3.6445	3.9697	-2.1697*
3.	Absenteeism due to emotional fatigue	2.6683	3.7144	-2.8343*
4.	Absenteeism due to physical fatigue	3.2454	4.2469	-3.1408*
5.	Absenteeism due to child care	3.1143	3.8339	-2.8032*
6.	Absenteeism due to elder' care	2.6569	2.4109	0.5918

* *Significant at five per cent level.*

The highly rated variables in absenteeism among the employees in PSBs are 'absenteeism due to family related problems' and 'physical fatigue' since their mean scores are 3.6445 and 3.2454 respectively.

Among the employees in PRBs, these two are absenteeism due to 'physical fatigue' and 'family related problems' since their mean scores are 4.2469 and 3.9697 respectively. Regarding the perception on variables in absenteeism, the significant differences among the employees in PSBs and PRBs have been identified in the case of absenteeism due to 'ill-health', 'family related problems', 'emotional fatigue', 'physical fatigue' and 'child care' since their '*t*' statistics are significant at five per cent level.

Reliability and Validity of Variables in Absenteeism

Before summarizing the scores of variables related to absenteeism, the reliability and validity of the variables in absenteeism are tested with the help of confirmatory factor analysis. The results are presented in Table 5.11.

Table 5.11: Reliability and validity of variables in absenteeism

Sl. No.	Variable in Absenteeism	Standardized Factor Loading	'*t*' statistics	Composite Reliability	Average Variance Extracted	Reliability Co-efficient
1.	Absenteeism due to ill-health	0.8844	5.3699*	0.7306	58.74	0.7704
2.	Absenteeism due to family-related problems	0.7439	3.2491*			
3.	Absenteeism due to emotional fatigue	0.7714	3.5084*			
4.	Absenteeism due to physical fatigue	0.8329	4.8633*			
5.	Absenteeism due to child-care	0.7104	3.3044*			
6.	Absenteeism due to elder care	0.6719	3.2668*			

* *Significant at five per cent level.*

The standardized factor loading of the variables vary from 0.6719 to 0.8844. All six standardized factor loadings are significant at five per cent level. The composite reliability of the construct is greater than the minimum threshold of 0.50. All these two results confirm the convergent validity of the construct. The average variance extracted by the construct is greater than the standard minimum of

50 which reveals the convergent validity. The reliability co-efficient of the construct shows that the included six variables in absenteeism explain the construct to the extent of 77.04 per cent. Hence, the six variables have been included for the estimation of absenteeism among the employees.

Score on Level of Absenteeism (LOA) among the Employees

The level of absenteeism among the employees, has been measured with the help of the mean scores of the variables in absenteeism. The level of absenteeism among the employees is confined to less than 2.00; 2.00 to 3.00; 3.01 to 4.00 and above 4.00. Table 5.12 explains the distribution of employees on the basis of their LOA.

Table 5.12: Score on level of absenteeism (LOA) among the employees

Sl.No.	LOA	Number of Employees in		Total
		PSBs	PRBs	
1.	Less than 2.00	65(20.97)	13(11.71)	78(18.52)
2.	2.00 - 3.00	109(35.16)	21(18.92)	130(30.88)
3.	3.01 - 4.00	111(35.81)	48(43.24)	159(37.77)
4.	Above 4.00	25(8.06)	29(26.13)	54(12.83)
	Total	**310(100)**	**111(100)**	**421(100)**

Note: Figures in brackets indicate percentage

The important LOA among the employees are 3.01 to 4.00 and 2.00 to 3.00 which constitute 37.77 and 30.88 per cent of their respective total. The employees with the LOA of above 4.00 constitute 12.83 per cent of the total. The important LOA among the employees in PSBs are 3.01 to 4.00 and 2.00 to 3.00 which constitute 35.81 and 35.16 per cent of their respective total. Among the employees in PRBs, these are 3.01 to 4.00 and above 4.00 which constitute 43.24 and 26.13 per cent of their respective total. The analysis infers that the LOA is higher among the PRBs than in PSBs.

FAMILY OUTCOME AMONG THE EMPLOYEES

The work-family conflict and family-work conflict may generate some family outcomes. The degree of family outcomes of these conflicts may be in different forms. The present study covers only positive parenting, family integration, parental satisfaction, family adaptation and family satisfaction. The about above said outcomes have been measured with the help of some factors.

Positive Parenting among the Employees

One of the family outcomes of the work-family imbalance is positive parenting. It indicates the level of understanding and enjoyment in being the parent of the family. Since the positive parenting has it's an influence on the job performance, it is included as one of the family outcome variables. Eventhough there one so many statements to measure the positive parenting, the present study is confined to only five statements namely very often laugh together with my children, always listen to my children's ideas and opinions, eat together as a family, make sure my children knew they were appreciated and know where my children are. The employees are asked to rate the statements at five point scale from highly agree to highly disagree. The scores assigned on these scales are from 5 to 1 respectively.

The level of positive parenting has been examined by the mean scores of the statements related to positive parenting. The mean scores of the five statements, related to positive parenting among the employees in PSBs and PRBs, have been computed separately to exhibit the level of positive parenting among the employees. The *'t'* test has been administered to find out the significant differences among the two groups of employees regarding positive parenting. The results are presented in Table 5.13.

Table 5.13: Mean score of positive parenting among the employees

Sl. No.	Statements	Mean Scores among Employees in		't' statistics
		PSBs	PRBs	
1.	Very often I laugh together with my children	3.3694	2.5411	2.3664*
2.	Always listen to my children's ideas and opinions	3.1362	2.6669	2.8024*
3.	Eat together as a family	2.5409	2.1623	1.2491
4.	Make sure my children know they are appreciated	3.0941	2.6217	2.7344*
5.	Know where my children are	3.1345	2.1776	2.9453*

* *Significant at five per cent level.*

Higher perception on positive parenting among the employees in PSBs are found in 'very often I laugh together with my children' and 'always listen to my children's ideas and opinions' since their respective mean scores are 3.3694 and 3.1362. Among the employees in PRBs, these are 'always listen to my children's ideas and opinions' and 'make sure my children know they are appreciated' since their mean scores are 2.6669 and 2.6217 respectively. Regarding the perception on positive parenting the significant differences among the two groups of employees have been noticed in the cases of 'very often I laugh together with my children', 'always listen to my children's ideas and opinions', 'make sure my children know they are appreciated' and 'know where my children are' since their respective *'t'* statistics are significant at five per cent level.

Reliability and Validity of the Statements on Positive Parents

The scores of these statements have been included to analyse the reliability and validity of statements in positive parenting with the help of Confirmatory Factor Analysis (CFA). The result of CFA is given in Table 5.14.

Table 5.14: Reliability and validity of the statements on positive parenting

Sl. No.	Statements	Standardized Factor Loading	't' statistics	Composite Reliability	Average Variance Extracted	Reliability
1.	Very often I laugh together with my children	0.8454	5.1043*	0.7917	59.69	0.8018
2.	Always listen to my children's ideas and opinions	0.8893	5.5432*			
3.	Eat together as a family	0.7506	4.1737*			
4.	Make sure my children know they are appreciated	0.7433	4.0291*			
5.	Know where my children are	0.7124	3.6733*			

* *Significant at five per cent level.*

The standardized factor loading of the statements in positive parenting varies from 0.7124 to 0.8893. The '*t*' statistics of the standardized factor loading of all statements are significant at five per cent level. It reveals the convergent validity of the construct. The composite reliability is greater than the minimum threshold of 0.50 which reveals the convergent validity. The average variance extracted by the construct is greater than the minimum threshold of 50 per cent which also indicates the convergent validity of the construct. The reliability co-efficient indicates that the included five statements explain the construct to the extent of 80.18 per cent. Hence, the five statements related to positive parenting have been included to represent the level of positive parenting.

Score on Level of Positive Parenting (LPP) among the Employees

The level of positive parenting among the employees with children is computed by the mean score of the variables in positive parenting. The LPP among the employees in the present study is confined to less than 2.00; 2.00 to 3.00; 3.01 to 4.00 and above 4.00. The distribution of employees on the basis of their LPP is given in Table 5.15.

Table 5.15: Score on level of positive parenting (LPP) among the employees

Sl.No.	LPP	Number of Employees in		Total
		PSBs	PRBs	
1.	Less than 2.00	80(29.96)	23(27.06)	103(29.26)
2.	2.00 - 3.00	103(38.58)	44(51.76)	147(41.76)
3.	3.01 - 4.00	69(25.84)	14(16.47)	83(23.58)
4.	Above 4.00	15(5.62)	4(4.71)	19(5.40)
	Total	**267(100)**	**85(100)**	**352(100)**

Note: Figures in brackets indicate percentage

The important levels of LPP among the employees are 2.00 to 3.00 and less than 2.00 which constitute 41.76 and 29.26 per cent of their respective total. The employees with the LPP of above 4.00 constitute 5.40 per cent of the total. The important LPP among the employees in PSBs are 2.00 to 3.00 and less than 2.00 which constitute 38.58 and 29.96 per cent of their respective total. Among the employees in PRBs, these two are also the same but constitute 51.76 and 27.06 per cent of their respective total. It is seen that, the levels of positive parenting is identified as higher among the employees in PSBs than among the employees in PRBs.

Family Integration among the Employees

Family integration represents the level of integration among the employees along with their family members. Since it is one of the family outcomes and also one of the factors influencing the job performance of the employees, it is included as one of the variables of family outcome. The family integration in the present study has been measured with the help of five statements. The employees are asked to rate these statements at five point scale, from highly agree to highly disagree according to the order of existence in their family.

The level of family integration among the employees has been measured by the mean scores of the five statements, related with family integration. The mean scores of the five statements and also the overall family integration among the employees in PSBs and PRBs have been computed separately to exhibit the level of family integration among the employees. Regarding the level of family integration, the significant differences among the two groups of employees have been examined with the help of '*t*' test. The results are shown in Table 5.16.

Table 5.16: Mean scores on statements on family integration among the employees

Sl. No.	Statements on Family Integration	Mean Scores among Employees in		'*t*' statistics
		PSBs	PRBs	
1.	Strong unity in my family	3.4184	2.6411	1.9908*
2.	Feeling of 'security' with my family members	3.3915	3.2292	0.2917
3.	Frequent participation in all the family functions	3.6668	3.1444	1.5645
4.	Frequent counselling with family members	3.5142	2.6629	2.5234*
5.	Participating in the matters of all the family members	3.4623	2.4162	3.2917*

* *Significant at five per cent level.*

The highly integrated family affairs among the employees in the PSBs are 'frequent participation in all the family functions' and 'frequent counselling with family members' since their mean scores are 3.6668 and 3.5142 respectively. Among the employees in PRBs, these are the 'feeling of 'security' with my family members' and 'frequent participation in all family functions' since their mean scores are 3.2292 and 3.1444 respectively. Regarding the family integration the significant differences among the two groups of employees has been noticed in the cases of strong unity in my family', 'frequent counseling with family members' and 'participating in the matters of all the family members' since their respective '*t*' statistics are significant at five per cent level.

Reliability and Validity of Statements on Family Integration

Five variables have been included to measure the family integration. In order to test the reliability and validity of the variables in this construct, the CFA has been used. The scores of the statements have been included to test the reliability and validity of the statements in the construct. The results are given in Table 5.17.

Table 5.17: Reliability and validity of statements on family integration

Sl. No.	Statements	Standardized Factor Loading	'*t*' statistics	Composite Reliability	Average Variance Extracted	Reliability
1.	Strong unity in my family	0.7268	2.5443*	0.7411	53.39	0.7608
2.	Feeling of 'security' with my family members	0.7944	3.0942*			
3.	Frequent participation in all family functions	0.8635	3.8187*			
4.	Frequent counselling with family members	0.7186	2.2408*			
5.	Participating in the matters of all the family members	0.7567	2.8184*			

* *Significant at five per cent level.*

Table 5.17 shows the result of confirmatory factor analysis. The standardized factor loadings range from 0.7186 to 0.8635. All the standardized factor loadings are significant at five per cent level.

The composite reliability of the construct is greater than the minimum threshold of 0.50. All these results reveal the convergent validity of the construct. The average variance extracted by the construct is also greater than 50 per cent which supports the previous result. The reliability co-efficient of 0.7608 of the construct indicates that the included seven statements explain the construct to the extent of 76.08 per cent. Hence, these five statements have been included to measure the family integration among the employees.

Score on the Level of Family Integration (LFI) among the Employees

The level of family integration, among the employees, has been computed by the mean score of the variables in family integration. The LFI, in the present study, is confined to less than 2.00; 2.00 to 3.00; 3.01 to 4.00 and above 4.00. The distribution of employees on the basis of their LFI is shown in Table 5.18.

Table 5.18: Score on level of family integration (LFI) among the employees

Sl.No.	LFI	Number of Employees in		Total
		PSBs	PRBs	
1.	Less than 2.00	60(19.35)	36(32.43)	96(22.81)
2.	2.00 - 3.00	81(26.13)	47(42.34)	128(30.40)
3.	3.01 - 4.00	108(34.84)	22(19.82)	130(30.88)
4.	Above 4.00	61(19.68)	6(5.41)	67(15.91)
	Total	**310(100)**	**111(100)**	**421(100)**

Note: Figures in brackets indicate percentage

The important levels of family integration among the employees are 3.01 to 4.00 and 2.00 to 3.00 which constitute 30.88 and 30.40 per cent of their respective total. The employees with the LFI of above 4.00 constitute 15.91 per cent of the total. The important LFI among the employees in PSBs are 3.01 to 4.00 and 2.00 to 3.00 which constitute 34.84 and 26.13 per cent of their respective total. Among the employees in PRBs, these two are 2.00 to 3.00 and less than 2.00 which constitute 42.34 and 32.43 per cent of their respective total. The analysis reveals that the LFI among the employees in PSBs is higher than that among the employees in PRBs.

Parental Satisfaction among the Employees

'Parental satisfaction' indicates the level of satisfaction among the employees as a parent of their children. Even though the variables related to parental satisfaction are too many, the present study has confined it to six variables. The married employees are asked to rate the above said six variables at five point scale from highly satisfied to highly dissatisfied. The scores assigned on these scales are from 5 to 1 respectively.

The level of parental satisfaction among the employees in PSBs and PRBs has been examined with the help of the mean score of the variables in parental satisfaction among them separately. The '*t*' test has been applied to test the significant differences among the two groups of employees. The results are given in Table 5.19.

Table 5.19: Mean score on variables in parental satisfaction among employees

Sl. No.	Variables in Parental Satisfaction	Mean Scores among Employees in		't' statistics
		PSBs	PRBs	
1.	Parenting role	3.6171	2.5159	2.6244*
2.	Children's behaviour	3.5224	3.3068	0.9146
3.	Relationship with children	3.9119	3.2179	2.1037*
4.	Achievements of the children	3.6983	3.0944	2.0144*
5.	Ability to control the children	3.8908	3.2391	1.9969*
6.	Inter-relationship between the children	3.2291	3.2041	0.1134

* *Significant at five per cent level.*

The variables showing high satisfaction among the employees in PSBs are 'relationship with children' and 'ability to control the children' since their mean scores are 3.9119 and 3.8908 respectively. Among the employees in PRBs, these two are 'children's behaviour' and 'ability to control the children' since their mean scores are 3.3068 and 3.2391 respectively. Regarding the level of parental satisfaction, the significant differences among the employees in PSBs and PRBs have been noticed in the case of 'parenting role', 'relationship with children', 'achievements of the children' and 'ability to control the children' since their respective *'t'* statistics are significant at five per cent level.

Reliability and Validity of Variables in Parental Satisfaction

The scores of the variables related to parental satisfaction have been included for confirmatory factor analysis to analyse the reliability and validity of the variables included in parental satisfaction. The results are given in Table 5.20.

Table 5.20: Reliability and validity of variables in parental satisfaction

Sl. No.	Variables in Parental Satisfaction	Standardized Factor Loading	't' statistics	Composite Reliability	Average Variance Extracted	Reliability
1.	Parenting role	0.9147	4.1089*	0.7332	58.91	0.7593
2.	Children's behaviour	0.8233	3.5643*			
3.	Relationship with children	0.7908	3.3321*			
4.	Achievements of the children	0.7507	2.9099*			
5.	Ability to control the children	0.8662	3.7664*			
6.	Inter relationship between the children	0.7732	2.1144*			

* *Significant at five per cent level.*

The standardized factor loading of the variables in parental satisfaction is greater than 0.60 and all standardized factor loading are significant at five per cent level which reveals the convergent validity of the construct. The composite reliability is greater than the minimum threshold of 0.50. The average variance extracted by the construct is greater than 50 per cent, which also indicates the convergent validity of the construct. The reliability co-efficient of 0.7593 reveals that the included six variables in parental satisfaction explain it to the extent of 75.93 per cent. Hence, all the six variables in parental satisfaction have been included to measure the level of parental satisfaction among the employees.

Score on Level of Parental Satisfaction (LPS) among the Employees

The level of parental satisfaction among the employees has been computed by the mean scores of the variables in parental satisfaction. The LPS in the present study is confined to less than 2.00; 2.00 to 3.00; 3.01 to 4.00 and above 4.00. The distribution of employees on the basis of their LPS is shown in Table 5.21.

Table 5.21: Score on level of parental satisfaction (LPS) among the employees

Sl.No.	LPS	Number of Employees in		Total
		PSBs	PRBs	
1.	Less than 2.00	37(13.86)	11(12.94)	48(13.64)
2.	2.00 - 3.00	51(19.10)	39(45.88)	90(25.57)
3.	3.01 - 4.00	109(40.82)	21(24.71)	130(36.93)
4.	Above 4.00	70(26.22)	14(16.47)	84(23.86)
	Total	**267(100)**	**85(100)**	**352(100)**

Note: Figures in brackets indicate percentage

The important LPS among the employees are 3.01 to 4.00 and 2.00 to 3.00 which constitute 36.93 and 25.57 per cent of their respective total. The employees with the LPS of above 4.00 constitute 23.86 per cent of the total. The important LPS among the employees in PSBs are 3.01 to 4.00 and above 4.00 which constitute 40.82 and 26.22 per cent of their respective total. Among the employees in PRBs, these two are 2.00 to 3.00 and 3.01 to 4.00 which constitute 45.88 and 24.71 per cent of their respective total. The analysis reveals that the parental satisfaction is seen to the higher among the employees in PSBs than among the employees in PRBs.

Family Adaptation among the Employees

Family adaptation indicates the level of adaptation of the employees with the family members. Since family adaptation is one of the important family outcomes, it is included in the present study. The level of family adaptation among the employees has been measured with the help of six variables. The employees are asked to rate the given variables at five point scale on the basis of their level of adaptation from very high to very low. The level of family adaptation among the employees has been measured with the help of the mean scores of the variables in family adaptation among the employees in PSBs and PRBs. Regarding family adaptation, the significant differences among the two groups of employees have been examined with the help of *'t'* test. The results are presented in Table 5.22.

Table 5.22: Mean score on family adaptation among the employees

Sl. No.	Variables in Family Adaptation	Mean Scores among Employees in		*'t'* statistics
		PSBs	PRBs	
1.	Adaptation with partners	3.2149	2.3694	2.2494*
2.	Adaptation with the children	3.0616	2.9908	2.1541*
3.	Adaptation with other family members	3.2774	2.5606	1.9908*
4.	Adaptation with relatives	3.1411	2.3314	2.6517*
5.	Higher family responsibilities	3.0665	2.6944	1.2506
6.	Higher dependent population	3.1965	2.3094	2.3644*

* *Significant at five per cent level.*

Higher level of family adaptation is noticed in the cases of 'adaptation with other family members' and 'adaptation with partners' in PSBs since their mean scores are 3.2774 and 3.2149 respectively. In the case of employees in PRBs, the highly viewed family adaptation variables are 'adaptation with the children' and 'higher family responsibilities' since their mean scores are 2.9908 and 2.6944 respectively. Regarding the level of family adaptation, the significant differences among the two groups of employees have been noticed in the cases of adaptation with partners, with the children, other family members, relatives and higher dependent population since their respective *'t'* statistics are significant at five per cent level.

Reliability and Validity of Variables in Family Adaptation

The scores of the variables have been included for confirmatory factor analysis to test the reliability and validity of the variables in this construct. The results are given in Table 5.23.

Table 5.23: Reliability and validity of variables in family adaptation

Sl. No.	Variables in Family Adaptation	Standardized Factor Loading	't' statistics	Composite Reliability	Average Variance Extracted	Reliability
1.	Adaptation with partners	0.7739	3.1239*	0.7217	54.05	0.7414
2.	Adaptation with the children	0.6942	2.0014*			
3.	Adaptation with other family members	0.8663	3.7989*			
4.	Adaptation with relatives	0.8039	3.3345*			
5.	Higher family responsibilities	0.7241	2.5024*			
6.	Higher dependent population	0.6845	1.9941*			

* *Significant at five per cent level.*

The standardized factor loading ranges from 0.6845 to 0.8663. All standardized factor loadings are significant at five per cent since their respective *'t'* statistics are significant at five per cent level. The composite reliability of the construct is greater than 50 per cent, which reveals the content validity. The reliability co-efficient indicates that the included six variables explain the family adaptation to the extent of 74.14 per cent. Hence, the level of family adaptation is measured with the help of the included six variables.

Score on Level of Family Adaptation (LFA) among the Employees

The level of family adaptation among the employees has been measured with the help of the mean score of the variables in family adaptation. The LFA in the present study is confined to less than 2.00; 2.00 to 3.00; 3.01 to 4.00 and above 4.00. The distribution of employees on the basis of their LFA is given in Table 5.24.

The important LFA among the employees are 2.00 to 3.00 and 3.01 to 4.00 which constitutes 42.99 and 27.55 per cent of their respective total. The employees with the LFA of above 4.00 constitute 9.50 per cent of the total. The important LFA among the employees

Table 5.24: Score on level of family adaptation (LFA) among the employees

Sl.No.	LFA	Number of Employees in		Total
		PSBs	PRBs	
1.	Less than 2.00	54(17.42)	30(27.03)	84(19.96)
2.	2.00 - 3.00	119(38.39)	62(55.86)	181(42.99)
3.	3.01 - 4.00	105(33.87)	11(9.91)	116(27.55)
4.	Above 4.00	32(10.32)	8(7.20)	40(9.50)
	Total	**310(100)**	**111(100)**	**421(100)**

Note: Figures in brackets indicate percentage

in PSBs are 2.00 to 3.00 and 3.01 to 4.00 which constitute 38.39 and 33.87 per cent of their respective total. Among the employees in PRBs, these two LFA are 2.00 to 3.00 and less than 2.00 which constitute 55.86 and 27.03 per cent of their respective total. The analysis shows that the level of family adaptation is identified to the higher among the employees in PSBs than among the employees in PRBs.

Family Satisfaction among the Employees

Family satisfaction indicates the level of attitude towards the family members, family affairs and the way of solving family problems. Since family satisfaction is the pre-requisite for better job performance, it is included in the present study. The WFC and FWC may have their own influence on the family satisfaction. Hence, the present study has included it as one of the components of family outcomes. The family satisfaction among the employees has been measured with the help of 10 variables in the present study. The employees are asked to rate the 10 variables at five point scale from highly satisfied to highly dissatisfy.

The level of family satisfaction among the employees has been measured with the help of the mean scores of 10 variables among the employees in PSBs and PRBs. Regarding the level of family satisfaction, the significant differences among the two groups of employees have been analysed with the help of *'t'* test. The results are presented in Table 5.25.

Table 5.25: Mean score of family satisfaction among the employees

Sl. No.	Statements in Family Satisfaction	Mean Scores among Employees in		't' statistics
		PSBs	PRBs	
1.	Degree of closeness with family members	3.6978	2.5143	3.0914*
2.	Ability to cope with stress in the family	3.4682	2.6029	2.8549*
3.	Ability to be flexible in the family	3.5147	2.7233	2.4413*
4.	Ability to share positive experiences in the family	3.7344	3.0669	2.2109*
5.	Quality of communication between family members	3.2996	2.8145	1.4433
6.	Ability to resolve conflicts in the family	3.4544	2.5633	2.3917*
7.	Time spent with family members	3.1144	2.3949	2.2099*
8.	The way problems are discussed	3.6649	2.6647	2.9094*
9.	Fairness of criticism in your family	3.3947	2.5641	2.3241*
10.	Family members' concern for each other	3.2667	2.1517	3.4592*

* *Significant at five per cent level.*

Highly satisfied variables in family satisfaction among the employees in PSBs are found to the 'ability to share positive experiences' and 'degree of closeness with family members' since their respective mean scores are 3.7344 and 3.6978. Among the employees in PRBs, these variables are 'ability to share positive experiences' and 'quality of communication between family members' since their mean scores are 3.0669 and 2.8145 respectively. Regarding the level of satisfaction on variables in family satisfaction, the significant differences among the two groups of employees have been noticed in the case all variables, except 'quality of communication between family members' since their respective *'t'* statistics are significant at five per cent level.

Reliability and Validity of Statements in Family Satisfaction

The scores of the variables in family satisfaction have been included for the confirmatory factor analysis, in order to test the reliability and validity of the constructs. The results are given in Table 5.26.

Table 5.26: Reliability and validity of statements in family satisfaction

Sl. No.	Statements in Family Satisfaction	Standardized Factor Loading	't' statistics	Composite Reliability	Average Variance Extracted	Reliability
1.	Degree of closeness with family members	0.6939	3.1344*	0.7224	53.42	0.6909
2.	Ability to cope with stress in the family	0.7244	3.4565*			
3.	Ability to be flexible in the family	0.7459	3.6089*			
4.	Ability to share positive experiences in the family	0.7893	3.9961*			
5.	Quality of communication between family members	0.6868	3.1017*			
6.	Ability to resolve conflicts in the family	0.8445	4.0142*			
7.	Time spent with family members	0.8661	4.2549*			
8.	The way problems are discussed	0.8975	4.3884*			
9.	Fairness of criticism in your family	0.6884	3.1215*			
10.	Family members' concern for each other	0.7249	3.5089*			

* *Significant at five per cent level.*

The standardized factor loading of the variables in family satisfaction varies from 0.6884 to 0.8975. The standardized factor loading of all the variables are significant at five per cent level. The composite reliability is greater than the minimum threshold of 0.5. Both these two results confirm the convergent validity of the construct. The average variance extracted by the construct is greater than 50, which also reveals the convergent validity. The reliability co-efficient of the construct reveals that the included 10 variables explain the family satisfaction to the extent of 69.09 per cent. Hence, the 10 variables are included to measure the family satisfaction among the employees.

Score on Level of Family Satisfaction (LFS) among the Employees

The level of family satisfaction among the employees is measured by the mean score of the variables in family satisfaction. The LFA in the present study is confined to less than 2.00; 2.00 to 3.00; 3.01 to 4.00 and above 4.00. The distribution of employees on the basis of their LFA is given in Table 5.27.

Table 5.27: Score on level of family satisfaction (LFS) among the employees

Sl.No.	LFS	Number of Employees in		Total
		PSBs	PRBs	
1.	Less than 2.00	64(20.64)	13(11.71)	77(18.29)
2.	2.00 - 3.00	65(20.97)	57(51.35)	122(28.98)
3.	3.01 - 4.00	134(43.23)	29(26.13)	163(38.72)
4.	Above 4.00	47(15.16)	12(10.81)	59(14.01)
	Total	**310(100)**	**111(100)**	**421(100)**

Note: Figures in brackets indicate percentage

The important LFS among the employees are 3.01 to 4.00 and 2.00 to 3.00 which constitute 38.72 and 28.98 per cent of their respective total. The employees with the LFA of above 4.00 constitute 14.01 per cent of the total. The important LFS among the employees in PSBs are 3.01 to 4.00 and 2.00 to 3.00 which constitute 43.23 and 20.97 per cent of their respective total. Among the employees in PRBs, these two LFS are 2.00 to 3.00 and 3.01 to 4.00 which constitute 51.35 and 26.13 per cent of their respective total. The analysis infers that the LFS among the employees in PSBs greater than among the employees in PRBs.

LIFE SATISFACTION AMONG THE EMPLOYEES

Life satisfaction indicates the level of satisfaction on various aspects in life. Since life satisfaction is one of the employment outcomes, it has been included in the present study. The level of life satisfaction among the employees in the present study has been measured with the help of five statements. The employees are asked to rate these statements at five point scale from very high to very low according to the order of existence in their life. The scores assigned on this scales are from 5 to 1 respectively. The level of life satisfaction among the employees has been measured by the mean score of the five statements related to life satisfaction among the employees in PSBs and PRBs. Regarding the level of life satisfaction, the significant differences among the two groups of employees have been analysed with the help of *'t'* statistics. The results are given in Table 5.28.

Table 5.28: Mean score of statements in life satisfaction

Sl. No.	Statements in Life Satisfaction	Mean Scores among Employees in		't' statistics
		PSBs	PRBs	
1.	In most ways my life is close to my ideal	3.6743	3.0411	1.7891
2.	The conditions of my life are excellent	3.4141	2.3962	2.5192*
3.	I am satisfied with my life	3.5042	2.4145	2.8196*
4.	So far I have got the important things I want in life	3.0917	2.2141	2.7108*
5.	If I could live my life again, I would change almost nothing	3.5049	2.6143	2.6364*

** Significant at five per cent level.*

The highly perceived statements related to life satisfaction among the employees in PSBs are 'In most ways my life is close to my ideal' and. 'If I could live my life again, I would change almost nothing' since their mean scores are 3.6743 and 3.5049 respectively. Among the employees in PRBs, this is, 'In most ways my life is close to my ideal' since its mean score is 3.0411. Regarding the level of life satisfaction the significant differences among the two groups of employees have been found in the case of the conditions of 'my life are excellent', 'I am satisfied with my life', 'so far I have got the important things I want in life' and 'If I could live my life again, I would change almost nothing' since their respective *'t'* statistics are significant at five per cent level.

Reliability and Validity of Statement in Life Satisfaction

The scores of the statements have been included for confirmatory factor analysis to test the reliability and validity of the construct. The results are given in Table 5.29.

Table 5.29: Reliability and validity of statements related to life satisfaction

Sl. No.	Statements	Standardized Factor Loading	't' statistics	Composite Reliability	Average Variance Extracted	Reliability
1.	In most ways my life is close to my ideal	0.9233	4.2455*	0.7996	59.17	0.8103
2.	The conditions of my life are excellent	0.8409	3.5404*			
3.	I am satisfied with my life	0.7948	2.9145*			
4.	So far I have got the important things I want in life	0.7255	2.2454*			
5.	If I could live my life again, I would change almost nothing	0.7885	2.7332*			

* *Significant at five per cent level.*

The standardized factor loading of the statements vary from 0.7255 to 0.9233 whereas all standardized factor loadings are significant at five per cent level. The composite reliability of the construct is greater than the minimum threshold of 0.50. All these confirm the convergent validity of the construct. The average variance extracted by the construct is greater than 50 per cent which also proves the convergent validity of the construct. The reliability co-efficient of the construct reveals that the included five statements explain the life satisfaction factor to the extent of 81.03 per cent. Hence, the eight statements have been included to measure the level of life satisfaction among the employees.

Score on Level of Satisfaction among the Employees

The level of life satisfaction among the employees has been measured by the mean scores of the variables in life satisfaction. The score on life satisfaction (SLS) among the employees is confined to less than 2.00; 2.00 to 3.00; 3.01 to 4.00 and above 4.00. The distribution of employees on the basis of their SLS is given in Table 5.30.

Table 5.30: Score on life satisfaction (SLS) among the employees

Sl. No.	SLS	Mean Scores among Employees in		Total
		PSBs	PRBs	
1.	Less than 2.00	29(9.35)	19(17.12)	48(11.40)
2.	2.00 - 3.00	66(21.29)	68(61.26)	134(31.83)
3.	3.01 - 4.00	142(45.81)	16(14.41)	158(37.53)
4.	Above 4.00	73(23.55)	8(7.21)	81(19.24)
	Total	**310(100)**	**111(100)**	**421(100)**

Note: Figures in brackets indicate percentage

The important SLS among the employees are 3.01 to 4.00 and 2.00 to 3.00 which constitutes 37.53 and 31.83 per cent of their respective total. The employees with the SLS of above 4.00 constitute 19.24 per cent of the total. The important SLS among the employees in PSBs are 3.01 to 4.00 and above 4.00 which constitute 45.81 and 23.55 per cent of their respective total. Among the employees in PRBs, these two SLS are 2.00 to 3.00 and less than 2.00 which constitute 61.26 and 17.12 per cent of their respective total. The analysis reveals that the level of life satisfaction among the employees in PSBs is higher than among the employees in PRBs.

References

1. Frone, M.R., Russell, M. and Cooper, M.L. (1992), "Antecedents and Outcomes of Work-family Conflict: Testing a Model of the Work-family Interface", *Journal of Applied Psychology*, 21(3): 65-78.
2. Bedeian, A.G., Burke, B.G. and Moffest, R.G. (1988), "Outcomes of Work-family Conflict among Married Male and Female Professionals", *Journal of Management,* 14 (1): 475-491.
3. Burden, D.S. and Goozins, B. (1987), *Boston University Balancing Job and Home Life Study*, Boston: Boston University School of Social Work.
4. Aryee, S. (1992), "Antecedents and Outcomes of Work-family Conflict among Married Professional Women: Evidence from Singapore", *Human Relations,* 45(6): 813-837.
5. Judge, T.A., Boudrean, J.W. and Bretz, R.D. (1994), "Job and Life Attitudes of Male Employees", *Journal of Applied Psychology,* 79(6): 767-782.

6. Higgins, C.A., and Duxbury, L.E., (1992), "Work-family Conflict: A Comparison of Dual Career and Traditional-career Men", *Journal of Organizational Behaviour,* 13(1): 389-411.
7. Boles, J.S., Johnston, M.W. and Hair, (1997), "Role Stress, Work-family Conflict and Emotional Exhaustion: Inter-relationships and Effects on Some Work-related Consequences", *Journal of Personal Selling and Sales Management,* 17 (1): 17-28.
8. Low, G.S., Carvans, D.W., Grant, K. and Mon Crief, W.C., (2001), "Antecedents and Consequences Sales Person Burnout", *European Journal of Marketing,* 35(5&6): 587-611.
9. Keaveney, S.M. (1992), "An Empirical Investigation of Disfunctional Organizational Turnover among Chain and Non-chain Retail Store Buyers", *Journal of Retailing,* 68 (2): 145-173.
10. Miller, J.F., (2002), "*Motivating People*", Executive Excellence, December, p. 15.
11. Allen, T.D., Herst, D.E.L., Bruck, C.S., and Sulton, M. (2000), "Consequences Associated with Work-to-Family Conflict: A Review and Agenda for Future Research", *Journal of Occupational Health Psychology,* 5(2): 278-308.
12. Thomas, L.T. and Ganster, D.C., (1995), "Impact of Family-support Work Variables on Work-family Conflict and Strain: A Control Perspective", *Journal Applied Psychology,* 80(5): 6-15.
13. Goff, J., Mount, M.K. and Jamieson, R.L., (1990), "Employer Supported Child Care, Work-family Conflict, and Absenteeism - A Field Study", *Personnel Psychology,* 43 (1): 793-809.
14. Mac Ewen, K.E. and Barling, J., (1994), "Daily Consequences of Work Interference with Family and Family Interference with Work", *Work and Stress*, 8(1): 244-254.
15. Mc Donald, S. and Mac Intyre, P. (1997), "The Generic Job Satisfaction Scale: Scale Development and its Correlates", *Employee Assistance Quarterly*, 13(2): 1-16.
16. Chandraiah, K., Agarwal, S.C., Marimuthu, P. and Manoharan, N. (2003), "Occupational Stress and Job Satisfaction among Managers", *Indian Journal of Occupational and Environmental Medicine*, 7 (2): 6-11.
17. Beehr, T.A. and Newman, J.E. (1978), "Job Stress, Employee Health and Organizational Effectiveness: A Facet Analysis, Model and Literature Review", *Personnel Psychology*, 31(4): 69-74.
18. Parik, P., Tankari, A., Bhattacharya, T. (2004), "Occupational Stress and Coping among Ranges", *Journal of Health Management*, 6(1): 115-127.
19. Christine, A., Henle and Anita L. Blanchand (2008), "The Interaction of Work Stressors and Organizational Sanctions on Cyber Loafing", *Journal of Management Issues*, 20(3): 383-400.

6

Impact of Work-life Imbalance on the Coping Strategies for Work-life Balance

INTRODUCTION

The work-life imbalance may generate so many impacts on the employees' performance. It may be related to their family life, organizational performance and also their personal health. The researcher has made an attempt in the present study to analyse the impact of work-life imbalance (Work-family conflict and Family-work conflict) on a few variables namely organizational commitment, job satisfaction, job stress, absenteeism, positive parenting, family integration, parental satisfaction, family adaptation, family satisfaction and life satisfaction. The impacts have been measured for future policy implications.

Apart from this, the coping strategies, applied by the employees, to maintain their work-life balance have been focused upon, in this chapter. Since the coping strategies are highly essential to keep up the pace of employees' productivity and their organizational performance. The impact of social support factors, on the implementation of coping strategies by the employees, have been focused to exhibit the relative importance of social support among the employees to balance their work-life. The impact of coping strategies on the work-life imbalance has been examined to reduce both Work-family Conflict and Family-work Conflict among the employees.

IMPACT OF WORK-LIFE IMBALANCE ON ORGANIZATIONAL COMMITMENT

The work-life imbalance, in the present study, is analysed on the major factors of Work-family Conflict and Family-work Conflict.

It is imperative to analyse the impact of the two measurers on the organizational commitment of the employees. The multiple regression analysis has been executed to analyse this impact. The fitted regression model is

$$Y = a + b_1x_1 + b_2x_2 + e$$

Where

Y	–	Score on organizational commitment among the employees
X_1	–	Score on WFC
X_2	–	Score on FWC
b_1, b_2	–	Regression co-efficient of independent variables
a	–	Intercept and
e	–	Error term.

The impact of work-life imbalance on organizational commitment has been measured among the employees in PSBs, PRBs and also for pooled data. The results are shown in Table 6.1.

Table 6.1: Impact of work-life imbalance (WLI) on organizational commitment

Sl. No.	WLI Factors	Regression Co-efficient among Employees in		
		PSBs	PRBs	Pooled Data
1.	WFC	-0.1842*	-0.3454*	-0.2496*
2.	FWC	-0.0629	-0.2509*	-0.1022
3.	Constant	-0.4543	-1.1083	-0.7337
4.	R^2	0.8502	0.7314	0.8708
5.	F-statistics	12.4903*	8.4508*	13.9143*

** Significant at five per cent level.*

The significantly and negatively influencing work-life imbalance factor on organizational commitment among the employees in PSBs is WFC whereas in PRBs, these are WFC and FWC. A unit increase in the WFC and FWC would result in a decrease in organizational commitment of employees in PRBs by 0.3454 and 0.2509 units respectively. The changes in work-life imbalance factors, explain the changes in organizational commitment of the employees to a higher extent since its R^2 is 0.8708. The analysis reveals that the negative impact of WLI factors is higher among the employees in PRBs than in PSBs.

IMPACT OF WLI FACTORS ON JOB SATISFACTION

Job satisfaction is one of the important outcomes of work-life imbalance and also an important antecedent of the productivity of the employees. Hence, the study has made an attempt to analyse the impact of WLI on job satisfaction. The multiple regression analysis has been executed to analyse the impact. The dependent variable included in the present analysis, is the score on job satisfaction among the employees, whereas the independent variables are the score on WFC and FWC among the employees. The impact analysis has been measured among the employees in PSBs, PRBs and also for pooled data. The results are shown in Table 6.2.

Table 6.2: Impact of work-life imbalance factors on job satisfaction among the employees

Sl. No.	WLI Factors	Regression Co-efficient among Employees in		
		PSBs	PRBs	Pooled Data
1.	WFC	-0.2133*	-0.2508*	-0.2441*
2.	FWC	-0.1739*	-0.1569*	-0.1624*
3	Constant	-0.7036	-0.9332	-0.8144
4	R^2	0.7908	0.6817	0.8306
5	F-statistics	9.1703*	7.3539*	10.4564*

* *Significant at five per cent level.*

In the case of PSBs and PSBs, the WLI factors that significantly influence on job satisfaction, among the employees, are both WFC and FWC. The negative effect of WFC on job satisfaction among the employees in PRBs is higher whereas the negative effect of FWC on the job satisfaction among the employees in PSBs is higher. The analysis of pooled data reveals, the importance of both WFC and FWC on job satisfaction, since their regression co-efficients -0.2441 and -0.1624 are significant at five per cent level. The analysis reveals that the WFC and FWC have a significant negative impact on job satisfaction, among the employees. The changes in WFC and FWC explain the changes in job satisfaction to the extent of 83.06 per cent since its R^2 is 0.8306.

IMPACT OF WORK-LIFE IMBALANCE (WLI) ON JOB STRESS AMONG THE EMPLOYEES

Job stress is one of the important outcomes of the work-life imbalance. It also affects the level of productivity of employees and the organization. Hence, the present study has made an attempt to analyse the impact of WFC and FWC on job stress among the employees for some policy implications. The multiple regression analysis has been executed to analyse this impact. The results are given in Table 6.3.

Table 6.3: Impact of work-life imbalance (WLI) on job stress among the employees

Sl. No.	WLI Factors	Regression Co-efficient among Employees in		
		PSBs	PRBs	Pooled Data
1.	WFC	0.3417*	0.5033*	0.3802*
2.	FWC	0.0802	0.2647*	0.1417*
3	Constant	0.7317	1.3038	0.9606
4	R_2	0.7822	0.6877	0.8142
5	F-statistics	8.1089*	7.3244*	9.3081*

* *Significant at five per cent level.*

The WLI factor that significantly influence on job stress among the employees in PSBs is WFC whereas in the case of PRBs, these are WFC and FWC since their respective regression co-efficients are significant at five per cent level. The analysis of pooled data reveals that a unit increase in the WFC and FWC would result in an increase in job stress among the employees by 0.3802 and 0.1417 units respectively. The changes in WLI factors explain the changes in job stress to the extent of 81.42 per cent since its R^2 is 0.8142.

IMPACT ON WLI FACTORS ON ABSENTEEISM AMONG THE EMPLOYEES

The absenteeism among the employees is one of the outcomes of work-life imbalance. In order to analysis the extent to which the

WFC and FWC influence absenteeism among the employees, the multiple regression analysis has been used. The included dependent variable is score on absenteeism among the employees. The impact of WFC and FWC on absenteeism has been examined among the employees in PSBs, PRBs and also for pooled data separately. The results are presented in Table 6.4.

Table 6.4: Impact of work-life imbalance on absenteeism among the employees

Sl. No.	WLI Factors	Regression Co-efficient among Employees in		
		PSBs	PRBs	Pooled Data
1.	WFC	0.0869	0.3917*	0.1803*
2.	FWC	0.1142	0.2203*	0.1211
3	Constant	0.2969	0.5184	0.4317
4	R^2	0.4334	0.7815	0.7903
5.	F-statistics	5.0869	7.9963*	8.3442*

** Significant at five per cent level.*

Both the WFC and FWC have no significant impact on absenteeism among the employees in PSBs. In the case of PRBs, a unit increase in the WFC and FWC would result in an increase in absenteeism by 0.3917 and 0.2203 units respectively. The analysis of pooled data shows that a unit increase in WFC would result in an increase in absenteeism by 0.1803 units. The change in WFC and FWC explain the changes in absenteeism among the employees to the extent of 79.03 per cent.

IMPACT OF WORK-LIFE IMBALANCE ON POSITIVE PARENTING

Positive parenting is highly essential for a balanced family life. The work-life imbalance among the women employees may affect their positive parenting which may lead to Family-work Conflict. Hence, the present study has made an attempt to analyse the impact of WLI on positive parenting with the help of multiple regression analysis. The impact has been measured among the employees in PSBs, PRBs and also for pooled data. The results are shown in Table 6.5.

Table 6.5: Impact of work-life imbalance on positive parenting

Sl. No.	WLI Factors	Regression Co-efficient among Employees in		
		PSBs	PRBs	Pooled Data
1.	WFC	-0.0845	-0.2703*	-0.1708*
2.	FWC	-0.1339*	-0.3456*	-0.2517*
3	Constant	-0.2445	-0.8961	-0.5949
4	R^2	0.7914	0.6433	0.8316
5	F-statistics	8.4813*	7.0334*	9.1144*

* *Significant at five per cent level.*

The significantly and negatively influencing WLI factor among the employee in PSBs is FWC whereas in PRBs, these are both WFC and FWC. The analysis of pooled data reveals that a unit increase in the WFC and FWC would result in a decrease in positive parenting by 0.1708 and 0.2517 unit respectively. The changes in WLI factors explain the changes in positive parenting among the employees to the extent of 83.16 per cent.

IMPACT OF WLI FACTORS ON FAMILY INTEGRATION

Family integration represents the way in which the employees are integrating with their family members. It is one of the important family outcomes of the work-life imbalance and hence, included as one of the dependable variables in the present study. The impact of Work-life Imbalance (WLI) on the family integration among the employees in PSBs, PRBs and also for pooled data has been computed with the help of multiple regression analysis. The results are shown in Table 6.6.

Table 6.6: Impact of work-life imbalance on family integration among the employees

Sl. No.	WLI Factors	Regression Co-efficient among Employees in		
		PSBs	PRBs	Pooled Data
1.	WFC	-0.2739*	-0.4145*	-0.3446*
2.	FWC	-0.0911	-0.1033	-0.0993
3	Constant	-0.3442	-0.6862	-0.7141
4	R^2	0.8549	0.7149	0.8646
5	F-statistics	10.3342*	7.8442*	11.2449*

* *Significant at five per cent level.*

In both PSBs and PRBs, the significantly and negatively influencing WLI factor on family integration among the employees is WFC. A unit increase in the WFC would result in a decrease in family integration by 0.2739 and 0.4145 units in PSBs and PRBs respectively. The analysis of pooled data also reveals the significant negative impact of WFC on family integration. The changes in WLI factors explain the changes in family integration to the extent of 86.46 per cent.

IMPACT OF WLI FACTORS ON PARENTAL SATISFACTION AMONG THE EMPLOYEES

'Parental satisfaction' among the employees is treated as the dependent variable whereas the WFC and FWC are treated as independent variables. The multiple regression analysis has been used to analyse the impact of WLI factors on parental satisfaction among the employees in PSBs and PRBs. The results are illustrated in Table 6.7.

Table 6.7: Impact of work-life imbalance on parental satisfaction among the employees

Sl. No.	WLI Factors	Regression Co-efficient among Employees in		
		PSBs	PRBs	Pooled Data
1.	WFC	-0.1917*	-0.3108*	-0.2517*
2.	FWC	0.0244	-0.2456*	-0.1646*
3	Constant	-0.3342	-0.8108	-0.5685
4	R^2	0.7947	0.7089	0.8144
5	F-statistics	8.1408*	7.2306*	8.0849*

** Significant at five per cent level.*

A unit increase in the WFC among the employees in PSBs would result in a decline in parental satisfaction by 0.1917 units. In the case of PRBs, a unit increase in WFC and FWC would result in a decrease in parental satisfaction by 0.3108 and 0.2456 units respectively. The analysis of pooled data shows the importance of both WFC and FWC on parental satisfaction, among the employees. The co-efficient of determination indicates that the changes in WLI factors explain the changes in parental satisfaction to the extent of 81.44 per cent.

IMPACT OF WLI FACTORS ON FAMILY ADAPTATION

Family adaptation is one of the family outcomes of the work-life imbalance among the employees. It is imperative to analyses the impact of WLI factors on the family adaptation among the employees for some implication. The multiple regression analysis has been used to measure the impact. The included dependent variable is score on family adaptation among the employees. The results of regression analysis among the employees in PSBs, PRBs and also for pooled data are shown in Table 6.8.

Table 6.8: Impact of work-life imbalance on family adaptation among the employees

Sl. No.	WLI Factors	Regression Co-efficient among Employees in		
		PSBs	PRBs	Pooled Data
1.	WFC	-0.0965	-0.2916*	-0.2282*
2.	FWC	-0.0333	-0.3117*	-0.1708*
3	Constant	0.2456	-0.8708	-0.3868
4	R^2	0.3144	0.7962	0.8144
5	F-statistics	3.0642	8.9145*	9.6617*

* *Significant at five per cent level.*

Only in PRBs, the WLI factors have a significant negative impact on family adaptation. A unit increase in WFC and FWC would result in a decrease in family adaptation by 0.2916 and 0.3117 units respectively. The changes in WLI factors explain the changes in family adaptation, among the employees in PRBs, to the extent of 79.62 per cent. The analysis of pooled data also reveals the significant impact of WFC and FWC on family adaptation among the employees.

IMPACT OF WLI FACTORS ON FAMILY SATISFACTION AMONG THE EMPLOYEES

Family satisfaction is a prerequisite for work-life balance among the employees and also their organizational performance. The work-life imbalance may affect the family satisfaction. The present study has made an attempt to analyse the impact of WLI factors on family satisfaction among the employees with the help of multiple regression analysis. The impact of WLI factors has been examined among the employees in PSBs, PRBs and also for pooled data respectively. The results are given in Table 6.9.

Table 6.9: Impact of work-life imbalance on family satisfaction among the employees

Sl. No.	WLI Factors	Regression Co-efficient among Employees in		
		PSBs	PRBs	Pooled Data
1.	WFC	-0.2817*	-0.4156*	-0.3828*
2.	FWC	-0.1004	-0.3965*	-0.2736*
3	Constant	0.4817	-0.9937	-0.6836
4	R^2	0.7302	0.6969	0.7949
5	F-statistics	8.1081*	7.9646*	9.1232*

* *Significant at five per cent level.*

In the PSBs, the significantly influencing WLI factor on the family satisfaction is only WFC whereas in PRBs, these are WFC and FWC. In both cases, the WLI factors have negative influence on family satisfaction. The analysis of pooled data reveals that a unit increase in WFC and FWC results in a decline in family satisfaction by 0.3828 and 0.2736 units respectively. The changes in WFC and FWC explain the changes in family satisfaction to the extent of 79.49 per cent since its R^2 is 0.7949.

IMPACT OF WORK-LIFE IMBALANCE ON LIFE SATISFACTION

Life satisfaction among the employees has been measured with the help of score on life satisfaction. The ultimate aim of any person is life satisfaction. Whether this satisfaction is attained by the employees or not, has been discussed in the present analysis. The included dependent variable in the present analysis, is life satisfaction. The multiple regression analysis has been executed to analyse the impact of WLI on life satisfaction among the employees in PSBs, PRBs and also for pooled data. The results are given in Table 6.10. (*See table on next page*)

A unit increase in WLI factors results in a decrease in life satisfaction among the employees in PSBs by 0.2433 and 0.1265 units respectively. In the case of PRBs, it results in a decrease in life satisfaction by 0.4108 and 0.3269 units respectively. The analysis of pooled data also indicates that the WFC and FWC are having a significant and negative impact on life satisfaction. The changes in WLI factors explain the changes in life satisfaction to the extent of 86.46 per cent since its R^2 is 0.8646.

Table 6.10: Impact of work-life imbalance on life satisfaction among the employees

Sl. No.	WLI Factors	Regression Co-efficient among Employees in		
		PSBs	PRBs	Pooled Data
1.	WFC	-0.2433*	-0.4108*	-0.3917*
2.	FWC	-0.1265*	-0.3269*	-0.2683*
3	Constant	-0.6817	-1.2145	-1.0845
4	R^2	0.8145	0.7038	0.8646
5	F-statistics	10.3326*	8.1417*	11.9242*

* *Significant at five per cent level.*

STRATEGIES ADOPTED BY EMPLOYEES TO REDUCE WORK-LIFE IMBALANCE

One way to reduce work-family conflict is for individuals to have the ability to effectively cope with the stressful demands. Coping is the way in which the individual perceives her environment and stressors become positively changed. Effective coping styles should be associated with lower levels of perceived work-family conflict. There are multiple ways through which the individuals cope with the WFC and FWC. If an individual is effectively coping with her perceived WFC and FWC it would reduce her perceived conflict or even keep the conflict under their control. Individuals may take direct efforts to cope with work/ family conflict, and direct separate efforts to cope with family demands. Similarly, coping at home mostly would have direct impact on family Interference work conflict. The present study has made an attempt on the measurement of level of implementation of coping strategies to maintain the work-life balance among the employees.

Totally, eleven variables, related to coping, have been identified. The employees are asked to rate the level of implementation of coping variables at the work and family level, in five point scale from very high to very low. The mean scores of the level of implementation of coping variables among the employees in PSBs and PRBs have been computed separately. Regarding the level of implementation of coping variables, the significant differences among the two groups of employees have been analysed, with the help of '*t*' test. The results are given in Table 6.11.

Table 6.11: Coping variables of the work-life imbalances among the employees

Sl.No.	Statements	Mean Score among the Employees in		
		PSBs	PRBs	'*t*' statistics
1.	I tell myself that time takes care of situations like this	2.8185	2.0245	2.9917*
2.	I think that I have done well compared with others in similar situations	3.0233	2.2511	2.8044*
3.	I try to work harder and more efficiently	3.1456	2.7308	1.0516
4.	I consult with others to solve my problem	3.5087	3.0145	2.9103*
5.	I accept the situation thinking that there is little I can do to change it	3.2667	2.2916	2.2497*
6.	I tell myself that I can probably work things out to my advantage	2.7519	2.1445	2.0941*
7.	I know myself in my career	3.2298	2.3273	0.3962
8.	I try to avoid the stressful events to the maximum extent	3.4147	2.5914	2.8084*
9.	I perceive that this situation will change very soon	2.9699	2.2863	2.7403*
10.	I tackle the problems myself	3.6973	3.0144	2.9622*
11.	I request the help of my boss	2.5285	2.8411	-0.6694

** Significant at five per cent level.*

The highly adopted coping variables by the employees in PSBs are 'consultation with others to solve problems' and 'tackle the problem by themselves' since their mean scores are 3.5087 and 3.6973 respectively. Among the employees in PRBs, these two are also the same but with the mean score of 3.0145 and 3.0144 respectively. Regarding the application of coping variables, significant differences among the two groups of employees have been noticed in the case of eight coping variables out of eleven variables since their respective '*t*' statistics are significant at five per cent level.

IMPORTANT COPING STRATEGIES AMONG THE EMPLOYEES

The Exploratory Factor Analysis (EFA) has been administered to identify the important coping strategies among the employees. The score of eleven coping variables have been included for the analysis. Initially, the test of validity of data for factor analysis has been conducted with the help of KMO measure of sampling adequacy and Bartletts test of Sphericity. Both these two tests satisfy the validity of data for factor analysis since KMO measure is greater than 0.5 and the level of significance of chi-square is at zero per cent level. The result of EFA is shown in Table 6.12.

Table 6.12: Important coping strategies among the executives

Sl. No.	Coping Strategies	Number of Statements	Reliability Co-efficient	Eigen Value	Per cent of Variation Explained	Cumulative Per cent of Variation Explained
1.	Avoidance	3	0.7819	3.2445	26.44	26.44
2.	Positive thinking	3	0.8624	2.8173	20.26	46.70
3.	Direct action	3	0.7623	2.6244	18.19	64.89
4.	Help seeking	2	0.7695	1.8549	16.32	81.21
KMO measure of sampling adequacy: 0.8143				Bartletts test of sphericity: Chi-square value: 102.33*		

* *Significant at five per cent level.*

The EFA result in four coping strategies namely avoidance, positive thinking, direct action and help seeking. All the four strategies explain the coping variables to the extent of 81.21 per cent. The most important coping strategy is 'avoidance' since its eigen value and the per cent of variation explained is 3.2445 and 26.44 per cent respectively. The three coping variables included in this strategy explain it to the extent of 78.19 per cent since its reliability co-efficient is 0.7819.

The second and third important coping strategies are positive thinking and direct action which consist of three each coping variables with the reliability co-efficient of 0.8624 and 0.7623 respectively. The eigen value of these two strategies are 2.8173 and 2.6244 respectively. The per cent of variation, explained by these two coping strategies are 20.26 and 18.19 per cent respectively. The last coping strategy identified by the factor analysis is 'help seeking' since its eigen value and the per cent of variation explained by this strategy is 1.8549 and 16.32 per cent respectively. It consists of two coping variables with the reliability co-efficient of 0.7695. The factor analysis results in four important coping strategies adopted by the executives to tackle the WFC and FWC.

Reliability and Validity of Variables in Coping Strategies

The present study has made an attempt to analyse the reliability and validity of variables in coping strategies, with the help of Confirmatory Factor Analysis (CFA). The standardized factor loading of the variables, its '*t*' statistics, composite reliability and average variance extracted by each coping strategy are summarized in Table 6.13.

Table 6.13: Result of confirmatory factor analysis

Sl. No.	Coping Strategies	Range of Standardized Factor Loading	Range of '*t*' statistics	Composite Reliability	Average Variance Extracted
1.	Avoidance	0.9029-0.6817	3.7142*-2.4608*	0.7502	56.02
2.	Positive thinking	0.8936-0.7142	3.6568*-2.9147*	0.8144	58.99
3.	Direct action	0.9614-0.6214	4.1782*-2.3024*	0.7339	52.41
4.	Help seeking	0.9142-0.8114	3.8969*-3.0616*	0.7184	50.86

* *Significant at five per cent level.*

The '*t*' statistics of standardized factor loading of all variables in each coping strategy, are significant at five per cent level. It reveals the convergent validity of the construct. The composite reliability of the constructs is greater than the minimum threshold of 0.50 and the Average Variance Extracted is also greater than 50.00 per cent. These two results are also supporting the convergent validity. Hence, these two coping strategies have been included for factor analysis.

COPING STRATEGIES AMONG THE EMPLOYEES

The levels of application of coping strategies among the employees have been computed by the mean score of level of application of coping variables in each strategy. The mean score of the level of application of each coping strategy among the employees in PSBs and PRBs has been computed separately in order to exhibit the level of application of coping strategies. Regarding the level of application of coping strategies, the significant differences between the employees in PSBs and PRBs have been computed with the help of *'t'* test. The results are given in Table 6.14.

Table 6.14: Implementation of coping strategies with work-life balance

Sl. No.	Coping	Mean Score among Employees in		't' statistics
		PSBs	PRBS	
1.	Avoidance	3.6317	2.2678	2.8196*
2.	Positive thinking	2.9156	2.1666	2.9291*
3.	Direct action	3.3569	2.6842	2.3817*
4.	Help seeking	3.0686	2.9278	0.1508

* *Significant at five per cent level.*

The highly applied coping strategies among the employees in PSBs are 'avoidance' and 'direct action' since their mean scores are 3.6317 and 3.3569 respectively. Among the employees in PRBs, these two are 'help seeking' and 'direct action' since their mean scores are 2.9278 and 2.6842 respectively. Regarding the application of coping strategies, the significant difference among the two groups of employees have been identified in the case of coping strategies except 'help seeking' since their respective *'t'* statistics are significant at five per cent level.

Level of Implementation of Coping Strategies (LICS) among the Employees

The LICS among the employees have been computed by the mean score of the variables related to all coping strategies among the employees. The LICS in the present study is confined to less than 2.0; 2.00 to 3.00; 3.01 to 4.00 and above 4.00. The distribution of employees on the basis of their LICS, is given in Table 6.15.

Table 6.15: Level of implementation of coping strategies (LICS) among the employees

Sl.No.	LICS	Number of Employees in		Total
		PSBs	PRBs	
1.	Less than 2.00	25(8.06)	9(8.11)	34(8.07)
2.	2.00-3.00	84(27.10)	62(55.86)	146(34.68)
3.	3.01-4.00	136(43.87)	27(24.32)	163(38.72)
4.	Above 4.00	65(20.97)	13(11.71)	78(18.53)
	Total	**310(100)**	**111(100)**	**421(100)**

* *Significant at five per cent level.*
Note: Figures in brackets indicate percentage

The important LICS among the employees are 3.01 to 4.00 and 2.00 to 3.00 since they constitute 38.72, 34.68 per cent of their respective total. The employees with the LICS of above 4.00 constitute 18.53 per cent of the total. The important LICS among the employees in PSBs are 3.01 to 4.00 and 2.00 to 3.00 which constitute 43.87 and 27.10 per cent of their respective total. Among the employees in PRBs, these two are 2.00 to 3.00 and 3.01 to 4.00 which constitute 55.86 and 24.32 per cent of their respective total. The analysis reveals that the LICS is identified as higher among the employees in PSBs than among the employees in PRBs.

IMPACT OF SOCIAL SUPPORT ON LEVEL OF IMPLEMENTATION OF COPING STRATEGIES

The present study has made an attempt to measure the impact of social support on the LICS among the employees for some policy implication. The multiple regression analysis has been executed to analyse the impact. The fitted regression model is

$$Y = a + b_1x_1 + b_2x_2 + b_3x_3 + b_4x_4 + e$$

Where

y	–	LICS among the employees
x_1	–	Score on spouse support among the employees
x_2	–	Score on Domestic support among the employees
x_3	–	Score on support from supervisors among the employees
x_4	–	Score on support from co-workers among the employees
$b_1, \ldots b_4$	–	Regression co-efficients of independent variables
a	–	Intercept and
e	–	Error term.

Table 6.16: Impact of social supports on LICS among the employees

Sl. No.	Social Support Factors	Regression Co-efficient among Employees in		
		PSBs	PRBs	Pooled Data
1.	Spouse support	0.2845*	0.3028*	0.2731*
2.	Domestic support	0.1133	0.1309*	0.1039
3.	Support from supervisors	0.2949*	0.3441*	0.2842*
4.	Support from co-workers	0.0893	0.1114	0.0961
	Constant	1.2345	0.8968	1.0842
	R^2	0.8124	0.7393	0.8549
	F-statistics	10.2459*	8.8028*	12.6869*

* *Significant at five per cent level.*

Table 6.16 shows the regression co-efficients of social support factors on the LICS among the employees. The significantly influencing social support on LICS among the employees in PSBs are 'spouse support' and 'support from supervisors' whereas in PRBs, these are 'spouse support', 'domestic support' and 'support from supervisors', since their regression, co-efficients are significant at five per cent level. The analysis of pooled data reveals that a unit increase in the 'spouse support' and 'support from supervisors' would result in an increase in LICS among the employees by 0.2731 and

0.2842 units respectively. The change in social support factors explains the changes in LICS among the employees to the extent of 85.49 per cent.

IMPACT OF COPING STRATEGIES ON WFC AMONG THE EMPLOYEES

The coping strategies are highly essential to reduce the WFC among the employees. The present study has made an attempt to analyse the impact of implementation of various coping strategies on the WFC among the employees with the help of multiple regression analysis. The fitted regression model is

$$Y = a+b_1x_1+b_2x_2+b_3x_3+b_4x_4+e$$

Where

y	–	WFC among the employees
x_1	–	Score on avoidance among the employees
x_2	–	Score positive things among the employees
x_3	–	Score on direct action among the employees
x_4	–	Score on help-seeking among the employees
$b_1, \ldots b_4$	–	Regression co-efficient,
a	–	Intercept and
e	–	Error term.

Table 6.17: Impact of implementation of coping strategies on WFC

Sl. No.	Coping Strategies	Regression Co-efficient among Employees in		
		PSBs	PRBs	Pooled Data
1.	Avoidance	-0.0865	-0.1861*	-0.1435*
2.	Positive thinking	-0.1804*	-0.2442*	-0.2019*
3.	Direct action	0.0442	-0.0843	0.0143
4.	Help-seeking	-0.2441*	-0.2994*	-0.2193*
	Constant	0.1869	-0.6564	0.4108
	R^2	0.7969	-0.6865	0.8442
	F-statistics	9.1462*	8.1472*	10.8769*

* *Significant at five per cent level.*

Table 6.17 shows the regression co-efficients of coping strategies on WFC among the employees in PSBs and PRBs. The significantly negatively influencing coping strategies on WFC, among the employees in PSBs are 'positive thinking' and 'help seeking' whereas among the employees in PRBs, these are 'avoidance', 'positive thinking' and 'help-seeking'. The analysis of pooled data shows that a unit increase in the implementation of 'avoidance', 'positive thinking' and 'help-seeking' would result a decline in WFC by 0.1435, 0.2019 and 0.2193 units respectively. The changes in the implementation of coping strategies explain the changes in WFC among the employees, to the extent of 84.42 per cent.

IMPACT OF COPING STRATEGIES ON FWC AMONG THE EMPLOYEES

The impact of implementation of coping strategies on the FWC, among the employees has been analysed. The included dependent variable for the analysis is FWC among the employees and the included independent variables are score on the implementation of all 4 coping strategies. The impact has been measured among the employees in PSBs, PRBs and also for pooled data. The results are shown in Table 6.18.

Table 6.18: Impact of implementation of coping strategies on FWC

Sl. No.	Coping Strategies	Regression Co-efficient among Employees in		
		PSBs	PRBs	Pooled Data
1.	Avoidance	-0.0968	-0.2145*	-0.1349*
2.	Positive thinking	-0.1718*	-0.3908*	-0.2432*
3.	Direct action	-0.0811	-0.0996	-0.0731
4.	Help seeking	-0.3145*	-0.4512	-0.4096*
	Constant	-0.3345	-0.8546	-0.7139
	R^2	0.7408	0.7133	0.7963
	F-statistics	8.9147*	8.0844*	9.3445*

* *Significant at five per cent level.*

The significantly influencing coping strategies on FWC among the employees in PSBs are 'positive thinking' and 'help seeking' whereas in PRBs, these are 'avoidance' and 'positive thinking'. The analysis of pooled data reveals that a unit increase in the implementation of 'avoidance', 'positive thinking' and 'help-seeking' will result in a decline in FWC by 0.1349, 0.2432 and 0.4096 units respectively. The changes in the implementation of coping strategies explain the changes in FWC to the extent of 79.63 per cent.

Summary of Findings, Conclusion and Recommendations

INTRODUCTION

The present study focuses on three important aspects related to work-life imbalance among the women employees. At first, the profile of the employees and their social support has been examined to provide the background of the women employees. Secondly, the study has discussed the antecedents of work-life imbalances, the Work-family Conflict (WFC) and the Family-work Conflict (FWC) among the women employees. The third part of the study has examined the various outcomes of work-life imbalance, impact of WFC and FWC on these outcomes and also the level of implementation of coping strategies to maintain the work-life balance among the employees.

The confined objectives of the study are:

(i) to exhibit the socio-economic profile and social support of the employees;

(ii) to analyse the important antecedents of work-life imbalance among the employees;

(iii) to measure the work-family and family-work conflict among the employees;

(iv) to analyse the association between the profile, social support among the employees and their work-life imbalances;

(v) to examine the various outcomes of the work-life imbalances;

(vi) to evaluate the impact of work-life imbalance on the various outcomes of work-life imbalance; and

(vii) to analyse the level of implementation of coping strategies and its impact on the work-life imbalance among the employees.

In order to fulfill the objectives of the study, the essential data were collected with the help of pre-structured interview schedule. A pilot study was conducted among 50 women employees in the commercial banks, for the enrichment of the interview schedule. The census study has been conducted in the present study. The total number of women employees, working in public and private sector banks has been included for the present study. Totally, 372 and 152 women employees are working respectively in 117 and 34 public and private sector bank branches in this district. The appropriate statistical tools have been used to analyse the collected data. The results are discussed in the earlier chapters. This chapter includes the summary of findings, conclusions, and recommendations.

FINDINGS OF THE STUDY

The important age groups among the employees are 31 to 35 years and 36 to 40 years. The most important age groups among the employees in PSBs and PRBs are 36 to 40 years and 31 to 35 years respectively. The dominant levels of education among the employees are under graduation and post-graduation. The most important level of education among the employees in PSBs and PRBs is under graduation.

The dominant personal income groups among the employees are Rs. 25, 001 to 35,000 and Rs. 35, 001 to 45,000 per month. The most important groups of personal income per month among the employees in PSBs and PRBs are Rs. 35, 001 to 45,000 and Rs. 15, 000 to 25,000 respectively. The important years of experience among the employees are 9 to 12 years and 6 to 9 years. The most important years of experience among the employees both in PSBs and PRBs is 9 to 12 years. The years of experience among the employees in PSBs is greater than among the employees in PRBs.

The important marital status among the employees is 'married' which is commonly seen among the employees in PSBs and PRBs. The important type of family among the employees is nuclear family system. The important family size among the employees is 3 to 4 members and 5 to 6 members. The most important family size among the employees in both PSBs and PRBs is 3 to 4 members. The important number of earning members per family among the employees is two.

The dominant level of education of spouse among the employees is post graduation and engineering. The most important level of education of spouse among the employees in PSBs and PRBs is post graduation. Most of the spouses of the employees in both PSBs and PRBs are employed. Most of the married employees are having children in their family. The important age of the youngest child among the employees' family is 2 to 4 years and less than 2 years.

The dominant categories of family income per month among the employees are Rs. 35,001 to 45,000 and Rs. 45,001 to 55,000. The most important family income per month among the employees in PSBs and PRBs is Rs. 35, 001 to 45,000. The higher family responsibility among the employees in PSBs is child care and caring disabled child if any, and among the employees in PRBs, these two are also the same. Regarding the caring responsibilities, the significant differences among the employees in PSBs and PRBs have been noticed in the case of child care, caring of sick and disabled child.

The important time factors devoted to family work per day among the employees are 1 to 2 hours and 2 to 3 hours. The most important time spell devoted to family works per day among the employees in PSBs is 1 to 2 hours whereas among the employees in PRBs, it is 2 to 3 hours. The important designations among the employees are clerk and cashiers.

The dominant working hours in the banks, per day are 9 to 10 hours and 8 to 9 hours. The most important hours worked per day among the employees in PSBs is 8 to 9 hours whereas among the employees in PRBs, it is above 11 hours. Most of the employees are having regular working schedule. The highly irregular working schedules are seen among the employees in PRBs than among the employees in PSBs.

The highly perceived variables of spouse support among the employees in PSBs are 'interaction' and 'providing financial support' whereas among the employees in PRBs, these are 'sense of humour' and 'supportive for career development'. Regarding the perception on variables in spouse support, the significant differences among the two groups of employees have been noticed in the case of supporting in child care activities, household chores, financial support and interaction. The spouse support among the employees in PSBs is identified as higher than among the employees in PRBs.

The highly perceived variables in domestic support among the employees in PSBs are 'having people who care-for me' and 'frequent participation with my family members and friends' whereas among the employees in PRBs, these are 'emotional support is given by my relatives and friends' and 'having people who care-for me'. Regarding the perception on variables in domestic support, the significant differences among the employees in PSBs and PRBs have been noticed in four variables out of six variables.

The highly perceived variables in supervisors' support among the employees in PSBs are 'supervisor is a participative type' and 'supervisor is highly generous' whereas among the employees in PRBs, these area, 'supervisor is a participative type' and 'supervisor is highly generous'. Regarding the perception on variables in supervisors' support, the significant difference among the two groups of employees have been noticed in the case of all variables except 'supervisor understands my problem'. High level of supervisors' support is noticed among the employees in PSBs than among the employees in PRBs.

Among the employees in PSBs, the highly perceived variables in co-work support are 'highly informative' and 'responsibility sharing co-workers whereas' among the employees in PRBs, these are 'highly informative' and 'responsibility sharing co-workers'. Regarding the perception on variables in co-workers' support, the significant differences among the two groups of employees have been identified in all seven variables related to 'co-workers' support'. Higher level of co-worker support is identified among the employees in PSBs than among the employees in PRBs. The highly viewed variable of social supports among the employees in PSBs and PRBs is 'spouse supported'. Regarding the social supports, the significant differences among the two groups of employees have been identified in all four social supports. The level of social supports is identified as higher among the employees in PSBs than those in PRBs.

The important antecedents of work life imbalance, focused in the present study, are organizational role stress and work domain variables. The important factors in organizational role stress are lack of role autonomy, role ambiguity, role conflict and role overload. The highly viewed variables in lack of role autonomy among the employees in PSBs are 'higher rigidity in job' and 'no authority to allocate resources' whereas among the employees in PRBs, these are 'higher rigidity in the job' and 'no freedom to design the work schedule'. Regarding the perception on the variables in 'lack of role autonomy', significant differences among the two groups of employees, have been identified in the case of all six variables included. The level of lack of role autonomy is identified as higher among the employees in PRBs than those in PSBs.

The highly viewed variables in 'role ambiguity' among the employees in PSBs are ' lack of clarity of scope and responsibility in the job' and 'vagueness of role in the work' whereas among the employees in PRBs, these variables are 'not knowing the level of expectation of authorities' and 'lack of clarity of scope and responsibility in the job'. Regarding the perception on variables in 'role ambiguity', significant differences among the two groups of employees have been noticed in the case of all six variables included. The level of role ambiguity among the employees in PRBs is higher than among the employees in PSBs.

The highly viewed variables in 'role conflict' among the employees in PSBs are 'incompatible instructions from several people' and 'do not work in my excepted role'. Among the employees in PRBs, these two are 'incompatible instructions from several people' and 'do things acceptable by a few but not others'. Regarding the perception on variables in role conflict, significant differences among the two groups of employees have been identified in the case of all six variables. The higher level of role conflict has been identified among the employees in PRBs than among the employees in PSBs.

The highly viewed variables in 'role overload' among the employees in PSBs are 'too many supervisory hours' and 'I feel over-burdened in the role'. Among the employees in PRBs, these are 'feeling of being overburdened' and 'job assignments are very much taxing'. Regarding the perception on variables in 'role overload', the significant difference among the two groups of employees has been noticed in all six variables. The level of 'role overload' is higher among the employees in PRBs than those in PSBs.

The highly viewed role stressors among the employees in PSBs are 'role overload' and 'role ambiguity'. Among the employees in PRBs, these two are 'role overload' and 'lack of role autonomy'. Regarding the perception on role stressors, the significant difference among the two groups of employees has been noticed in all four role stressors and their level is higher among the employees in PRBs than those in PSBs.

The significantly associating profile variables with the level of perception on 'lack of autonomy' are age, educational qualification, personal income and years of experience whereas in the perception on 'role ambiguity', it is educational qualification. Regarding the perception on 'role conflict', the profile variables which are highly perceived are educational qualification, personal income and years of experience whereas in the perception on 'role overload', these profile variables are age and years of experience.

The significantly associating family domain variables with the perception on role stressors are 'caring responsibilities', and 'family income of the employees'. The important discriminant role stresses among the employees in PSBs and PRBs are role overload and role conflict which are higher among the employees in PRBs than in PSBs.

The highly viewed work domain variables for the work-life imbalance among the employees in PSBs are 'no balance between talents and salary' and 'poor empowerment in all aspects' whereas among the employees in PRBs, these are 'inconvenient working hours' and 'dumping of heavy work load'. Regarding the perception on work domain variables, the significant difference among the two groups of employees has been identified in the case of twenty variables out of 30 variables included.

The important work domain factors identified by the factor analysis are unsupportive colleagues, work pressure, performance inhibitors, lack of empowerment, effort-reward imbalance, working hours and working conditions. The highly perceived work domain factors for the work-life imbalance among the employees in PSBs are 'work pressure' and 'lack of empowerment' and in PRBs, these are also the same but the degree of attachment to these factors is comparatively higher among the employees in PRBs. Regarding the perception on these work domain factors, the significant difference among the two groups of employees has been noticed in six factors out of seven.

The significantly associating profile variables with the perception on work domain factors, among the employees, are their age and personal income whereas the family domain variables are time devoted to family work per day, caring responsibilities, and family size. The significantly associating organization domain variables are hours worked per day and working schedule. The important discriminant work domain variables among the two groups of employees are work pressure and working hours which are identified to the higher among the employees in PRBs than among the employees in PSBs.

The Work-family Conflict (WFC) among the employees, has been measured with the help of eight variables. The highly viewed variables among the employees in PSBs are 'stress leads to irritation at home' and 'my work keeps me away from my family activities more than I would like'. Among the employees in PRBs, the important variables are 'work affects the amount of time spent with family members' and 'work keeps the employees away from their family members'. Regarding the perception on variables related to WFC, the significant difference among the two groups of employees has been noticed in all eight variables. All the eight variables in WFC explain it to a reliable extent. The level of WFC is identified as higher among the employees in PRBs than among the employees in PSBs.

The Family-work Conflict (FWC) has been measured with the help of eight variables. The highly perceived FWC variables among the employees in PSBs are 'stress caused by children affects the work performance' and 'strained family relationship' whereas among the employees in PRBs, these two variables are 'strained family relationship' and 'family causes lack of concentration on work'. Regarding the perception on the variables related to FWC, the significant difference among the two groups of employees has been noticed in the case of four variables out of the eight variables. The included eight variables in FWC explain it to a reliable extent. Higher FWC is noticed among the employees in PRBs than among the employees in PSBs.

The profile variables significantly associating with the SWFC and SFWC, among the employees are age, educational qualification, personal income and years of experience of the employees. The family domain variables significantly associating with the perception on SWFC and SFWC are 'time devoted to family work per day', caring responsibilities, family income, age of the youngest child and marital status of the employees. The significantly associating organization variables with the SWFC and SFWC are hours worked per day and working schedule. The significantly correlating work domain variables with the WFC among the employees are unsupportive colleagues, work pressure, effort-reward imbalance and working hours whereas with the FWC, it is only work pressure.

The significantly influencing variables on the FWC among the employees in PSBs are working spouse, parental status, age of the youngest child, hours spend on household work, domestic support and spouse support whereas among the employees in PRBs, these variables are marital status, working spouse, caring responsibilities, hours spent on household work, domestic support and spouse support. The domestic and spouse support have a significant negative impact on FWC among the employees whereas the variables of marital status, working spouse, caring responsibilities and hours spent on household work have a significant positive impact on FWC.

The work domain and social support variables that significantly influence on WFC among the employees in PSBs are unsupportive colleagues, work pressure, working hours, supervisor's support and co-workers' support whereas among the employees in PRBs, these are unsupportive colleagues, work pressure, lack of empowerment, working hours, supervisor's support and co-workers' support. The supervisor's and co-workers' support have a significant negative impact on WFC among the employees whereas the variables of unsupportive colleagues, work pressure, lack of empowerment and working hours have a significant positive impact on WFC.

The significantly influencing role stresses and social support variables on WFC among the employees in PSBs are role ambiguity, role conflict, role overload, supervisor's and co-workers' support whereas among the employees in PRBs, these are lack of role autonomy, role conflict role overload, supervisor's and co-workers' support. The supervisor's and co-workers' support have a significant negative impact on WFC among the employees whereas the lack of role autonomy, role conflict and role overload have a significant by positive impact on WFC.

The consequence of work-life imbalance is measured by organizational commitment, job satisfaction, job stress, absenteeism, positive parenting, family integration, parental satisfaction, family adaptation, family satisfaction and life satisfaction. The highly perceived organizational commitment variables among the employees in PSBs are 'spending rest of the career in the bank' and 'emotional attachment with the bank'. Among the employees in PRBs, these two are 'spending rest of the career in the bank' and 'proud to be part of the bank'. Regarding the perception on the variables related to organizational commitment, the significant difference among the two groups of employees has been noticed in all seven variables in organizational commitment. The included seven variables in organizational commitment explain it to a reliable extent. The higher organizational commitment is identified among the employees in PSBs than those in PRBs.

Job satisfaction among the employees has been measured with the help of twelve variables related to job satisfaction. These twelve variables explain it to a reliable extent. The highly perceived variables in job satisfaction among the employees in PSBs are 'fringe benefits' and 'job security' whereas among the employees in PRBs, these are 'fringe benefits' and 'training and development'. Regarding the perception on the variables in job satisfaction, the significant difference among the two groups of employees has been noticed in the case of nature of work, organizational supervisor, relationship with co-workers, pay, fringe benefits, work load, job security, training and development opportunities, sorts of things they do and ability to meet career goals. The higher level of job satisfaction is noticed among the employees in PSBs than those in PRBs.

Job stress among employees has been measured with the help of eighteen variables. The highly viewed variables in job stress among the employees in PSBs are 'complexity of work' and 'too much responsibility' whereas among the employees in PRBs, these two are 'job insecurity' and 'less liberty'. Regarding the perception on variables in job stress, the significant difference among the two groups of employees has been noticed in the case of 16 variables out of 18. The included 18 variables explain job stress to a reliable extent. Higher level of job stress is identified among the employees in PRBs than among employees in PSBs.

Absenteeism among the employees has been measured with the help of six variables. These six variables explain absenteeism to a reliable extent. The highly viewed variables in absenteeism among the employees in PSBs are 'family related problems' and 'physical fatigue' whereas among the employees in PRBs, these two are 'physical fatigue' and 'family-related problems'. Regarding the perception on these variables, the significant difference among the two groups of employees has been identified in case of five variables out of the total six. Higher rate of absenteeism is seen among the employees in PRBs than among the employees in PSBs.

Positive parenting among the employees is measured with the help of five variables which reveals the reliability also. The highly perceived variable among the employees in PSBs is 'very often I laughed together with my children', whereas among the employees in PRBs, this is 'I listen to my children's ideas and opinions'. Regarding the perception on positive parenting, the significant difference among the employees in PSBs and PRBs has been identified in the case of four variables out of the total five. Higher level of positive parenting is seen among the employees in PSBs than among employees in PRBs.

Family integration among the employees is measured with the help of five variables. The included five variables in family integration explain it to a reliable extent. The highly perceived variable among the employees in PSBs is 'frequent participation in all family functions' whereas among the employees in PRBs, it is 'feeling of security with my family members'. Regarding the perception on variables in family integration, the significant difference among the two groups of employees has been identified in three variables out of the total five. Higher level of family integration is identified among the employees in PSBs than among employees in PRBs.

The parental satisfaction among the employees is measured with the help of six variables which shows the reliability also. The higher parental satisfaction is identified in the case of 'relationship with children' and 'ability to control the children' among the employees in PSBs. Whereas in PRBs, these are 'children's behaviour' and 'ability to control the children'. Regarding the perception on variable in parental satisfaction, the significant difference among the two groups of employees has been identified in the case of four variables out of the total six. Higher level of parental satisfaction is seen among the employees in PSBs than among the employees in PRBs.

Family adaptation among the employees has been measured with the help of six variables. All six variables in family adaptation explain it to a reliable extent. The highly viewed variables in family adaptation among the employees in PSBs are 'adaptation with other family members' and 'adaptation with partners' whereas among the employees in PRBs, these two are 'adaptation with the children' and 'higher family responsibilities'. Regarding the perception on variables in family adaptation, the significant difference among the employees in PSBs and PRBs has been noticed in five variables out of the total six. Higher level of family adaptation is seen among the employees in PSBs than among the employees in PRBs.

Family satisfaction among the employees is measured with the help of ten variables. The highly viewed variables among the employees in PSBs are 'ability to share positive experiences' and 'degree of closeness with family members' whereas among the employees in PRBs, these two are 'ability to share positive experiences' and 'quality of communication between family members'. Regarding the perception on the variables in family satisfaction, the significant difference among the two groups of employees has been identified in nine variables out of the total ten variables in family satisfaction. Higher level of family satisfaction is identified among the employees in PSBs than among those in PRBs.

Life satisfaction among the employees is measured with the help of five variables. These five variables explain it to a reliable extent. The highly perceived variables among the employees in PSBs are 'In most ways my life is close to my ideal' and 'if I could live my life again, I would change almost nothing'. Among the employees in PRBs, this is 'In most ways my life is close to my idea'. Regarding the perception on variables in life satisfaction, the significant difference among the two groups of employees is seen in four variables out of the total five variables. Higher level of life satisfaction is identified among the employees in PSBs than among the employees in PRBs.

The significantly and negatively influencing work-life imbalance factors on organizational commitment, among the employees in PRBs are Work-family Conflict (WFC) and Family-work Conflict (FWC) whereas in the case of PSBs, it is only WFC. The changes in work-life imbalance factors explain the changes in organizational commitment to a higher extent in PSBs than in PRBs. In both PSBs and PRBs, they significantly and negatively influence the job satisfaction among the employees.

Higher degree of positive significant influence of WFC and FWC on the job stress among employees has been noticed among the employees in PRBs than in PSBs. In the case of PSBs, the WFC has a significant positive impact on the job stress among the employees. The analysis of pooled data reveals the relative importance of WFC and FWC on the job stress among the employees. The WFC and FWC have a significant positive impact on absenteeism among the employees in PRBs whereas these two factors have no significant impact on absenteeism among the employees in PSBs.

Among the employees in PSBs, the significantly and negatively influencing factor on positive parenting is Family-work Conflict whereas among the employees in PRBs, these factors are both WFC and FWC conflicts. The degree of influence of the WFC and FWC on positive parenting among the employees in PRBs is identified to be higher than that among the employees in PSBs. The analysis of pooled data reveals the relative importance of WFC and FWC on positive parenting among the employees.

The WFC has a significant negative impact on the family integration among the employees in both PSBs and PRBs. But the degree of influence of WFC on family integration is higher among the employees in PRBs than in PSBs. Regarding parental satisfaction, the significantly and negatively influencing work-life imbalance factors among the employees in PSBs is WFC whereas among the employees in PRBs, they are both WFC and FWC. The analysis of pooled data reveals the relative importance of WFC and FWC on the parental satisfaction among the employees.

Regarding family adaptation, the significantly and negatively influencing work-life imbalance factors are both WFC and FWC among the employees in PRBs whereas among the employees in PSBs, these two factors namely WFC and FWC, have no significant impact on family adaptation. The analysis of pooled data reveals that there is a significant negative impact of WFC and FWC on family adaptation among the employees.

Among the employees in PSBs, the WFC has a significant negative impact on family satisfaction whereas among the employees in PRBs, both WFC and FWC have a significant negative impact on family satisfaction. The degree of negative impact of WFC and FWC on family satisfaction is identified as higher among the employees in PRBs than among employees in PSBs. The analysis of pooled data also reveals the relative importance of both WFC and FWC on family satisfaction among the employees.

Regarding life satisfaction, the significantly influencing work-life imbalance factors are both WFC and FWC. The degree of negative impact of WFC and FWC on life satisfaction is higher among the employees in PRBs than among employees in PSBs. The analysis of pooled data reveals that both WFC and FWC have a significant negative impact on life satisfaction among the employees.

The highly implemented coping variables among the employees in PSBs are 'consultation with others to solve the problems' and 'tackle the problem by them selves'. Among the employees in PRBs, these variables are also the same. Regarding the rate of implementation of coping variables, the significant difference among the two groups of employees has been noticed in eight variables out of the total 11 variables.

The important coping strategies identified by the factor analysis are avoidance, positive thinking, direct action and help seeking. The variables in each important coping strategy explain it to a reliable extent. The highly implemented coping strategies among the employees in PSBs are 'avoidance' and 'direct action' whereas among the employees in PRBs, these two are 'help seeking' and 'direct action'. Regarding the level of implementation of coping strategies, the significant difference among the two groups of employees has been noticed in three out of four coping strategies. The level of implementation of coping strategies among the employees in PSBs is higher than among the employees in PRBs.

The significantly and positively influencing social supports on the level of implementation of coping strategies among the employees in PSBs are 'spouse support' and 'support from supervisors'. Among the employees in PRBs, these are 'spouse' and 'domestic support' and 'support from supervisors'. The degree of influence of social support on the level of implementation of coping strategies is identified as higher among the employees in PRBs than among employees in PSBs. The analysis of pooled data reveals the relative importance of 'spouse support' and 'support from supervisors' in the level of implementation of coping strategies.

The significantly and negatively influencing coping strategies on the WFC among the employees in PSBs are 'positive thinking' and 'help seeking' whereas among the employees in PRBs, these are 'avoidance', 'positive thinking' and 'help seeking'. The analysis of pooled data also reveals that 'avoidance', 'positive thinking' and 'help seeking' are reducing the work-family conflict to a significant level.

In the PSBs, the significantly and negatively influencing coping strategies on the FWC among the employees are 'positive thinking' and 'help seeking' whereas among the employees in PRBs, these coping strategies are 'avoidance' and 'positive thinking'. The analysis of pooled data also reveals the relative importance of 'avoidance', 'positive thinking' and 'help seeking' in reduction of FWC among the employees.

CONCLUDING REMARKS

The present study concludes that the work-life imbalances are higher among the women employees especially in Private Sector Banks than in Public Sector Banks. The important causes for their work-life imbalance are lack of social support, organizational role stresses and their work domain variables. The work-life imbalances are not only affecting the organizational commitment but also their family satisfaction and life satisfaction. The level of implementation of coping strategies to maintain their work-life balance is higher among the employees in Public Sector Banks than in Private sector Banks. But the level of implementation of coping strategies by the women employees is significantly reducing their work-life imbalance. Even though, the productivity and profitability of the Private Sector Banks are high compared with Public Sector Banks, they are not good enough in maintaining their Human Resources which are essential for their survival and success. Hence the commercial banks are advised to implement suitable Human Resources management policies, in order to maintain the work-life balance among their employees.

SUGGESTIONS

Based on the findings of the study, the following suggestions are drawn:

Strategic Approach for Work-life Balance

Every commercial bank should have a good understanding of the importance of work-life balance among employees. These may include issues raised in employment-agreement negotiation, union consultations, the ongoing loss of, or failure to attract a particular group of employees, or the desire to be perceived as an employer of choice. Developing a work-life balance policy and practices is a strategic change process. There are five suggested stages of intervention:

(i) undertake work-life balance assessment and need analysis;

(ii) develop a strategic approach to work-life balance;

(iii) plan and implement a work-life balance plan;

(iv) evaluate the effectiveness of work-life balance initiatives; and

(v) review work-life balance needs and adopt a strategic approach. The following diagram depicts the strategic approach to work-life balance.

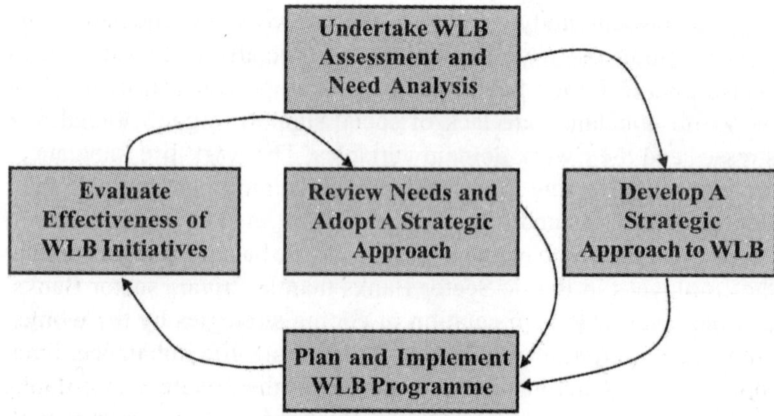

To resolve work life balance issues, they may be organized according to three themes. These themes are:

(i) The structural or contractual arrangements, as the specification of contracts in large projects may need to consider work-life issues up-front,

(ii) Formal and informal arrangements as there is a need for both formalized company policies (including flexible arrangements) that are accessible in practice together with informal arrangements at the worksite, and

(iii) Individual preferences need to be considered so that individuals can take some control over their working time habits while still meeting organizational imperatives.

Flexi-time Arrangements

Flexi-time arrangements may be permitted by the management for the women employees, in order to meet their family work requirements. Employees may be permitted to work a choice of additional working hours either before or after the regular working hours of 10 am to 5 pm, in order to compensate the loss of working hours. One employee might arrive early in the morning in order to leave earlier to pick up her school going children. Another employee might be a night owl who wishes to arrive at 10.00 am and work until 6 or 7 pm or even later.

HRM Policies

The adoption of work-family programmes is inevitable to solve the work-life imbalances. These programmes should cover six important aspects namely flexibility, leave arrangements, child care and elder care facilities, virtual office facilities, counseling and training, relevant to balance work and family.

Support from Spouse

A more egalitarian perspective of gender role would help to reduce working mothers' family demands. Men do not help out in housework because they are not taught to do so, and hence may not have skills in cooking or childcare. Men should be encouraged to take up family responsibilities, with appropriate training and counselling. This type of training should be given at their students' age, and only then only it will help them to develop a more egalitarian attitude towards gender role. In addition, hospitals or poly clinics can offer courses on baby care for both spouse and fathers-to-be and they should be strongly encouraged to participate so that they can help with childcare.

Full-day School

The long working hours of women employees contribute to a higher degree of job-parent conflict, which increases as children reach adolescence and parents become fearful of bad peer influence. Hence, full day school could be considered for primary, secondary and even at college levels. This would help to relieve the stress of working mothers, especially, the women employees who tend to work long hours. Full day schools allow students to be supervised by their teachers and enable them to engage in healthy activities in schools such as sports or school projects.

Good Marital Relationship

Job-spouse conflict has a great influence on the job, marital and life satisfaction of the women employees. Hence, it is important for them not to let their job affect their relationship with their spouses. The women employees are advised to spend more time with their spouse, in order to enhance their relationship. In addition, the women employees should show appreciation of their spouses' support in their profession, as spouse emotional support is an important asset for women employees.

Work-life Integration

Organization might help their employees to maintain an acceptable level of work-life balance by offering guidance on strategies, to help them maintain greater separation between the two domains. Schedule flexibility is a key for balancing the work-life among the women employees. This implies that the ability to adopt working hours to meet personal and/or family needs, may help employees cope with the competing demands of the work and non-work domains.

Family-support Work Environment

Top management of banks should be commited to establish and maintain the family-support work environments. This is important since research indicates that family-friendly programmes have been designed and introduced to meet business needs in lieu of meeting employee needs. The family-friendly programmes, include flexible work schedules, on-site child care, and family leave. Properly trained managers can create the culture that helps employees to balance their work requirements and also make the work itself less stressful.

Training Programmes

The training programmes of the banks should focus on the development of functional skills. After basic training, when an employee returns to her respective position the utilisation of skills is left to the initiative of the employee. With this realization, properly trained managers should provide on going training programmes which aim to teach employees how to manage time effectively. These ongoing training programmes should also aim to teach employees how to resolve problems associated with work-family and family-work conflicts.

Intrinsic Motivation

The present study demonstrates that intrinsic motivation decreases work-life imbalances and emotional exhaustion. It also increases employees' job performance, job satisfaction, and affective organizational commitment. In apparent recognition of these findings, managers should create high standards for service excellence, establish trust in employees, offer career opportunities and, where necessary, delegate authority, in order to enhance employees' intrinsic motivation and also their job performance, job satisfaction, and affective organizational commitment.

Special Leave to Women Employees Child-care Leave

Women employees may be granted special leave for atleast two years to bring up their new borns following the central government policy. The special leave or child care leave would ensure proper parental care and contribute to work-life balance. Similar special leaves should be granted for women employees, in case their children are to sit for public examinations, such as school final examination.

Introduction of Five-day Week

Introduction of five-day week, with a view to ensure more efficiency from the employees is suggested. This scheme will provide two whole days per week, for the employees to attend to family work, peacefully and contribute a lot to work-life balance. Several state government offices and public undertakings had been noticed, to register efficiency, after introduction of five-day week formula.

FUTURE RESEARCH DIRECTIONS

The present study opens scope for future research in the following directions:

The future research may focus on the linkage between work-life imbalance and emotional exhaustion among the employees. It can be extended to find out the impact of these imbalances and emotional exhaustion on job performance, job satisfaction and affective organizational commitment. A separate indepth analysis may be undertaken on the impact of intrinsic motivation among the employees and their work-life imbalance. The organizational culture and leadership in the banks and their role in work-life imbalance among the employees may be analysed in near future. The scope of the study may be extended to women employees in IT sector in future. The gender variation on work-life imbalance might be examined in future studies.

The linkage between social support and work-life balance may be focused for some future policy implications. Mentors appear to be an important factor in the development of work-life balance. Hence, future researches may be directed to examine the process by which mentors impact the work-life balance. Future research efforts should seek to expand this study and identity effective coping strategies for managing work-family conflict. The use of longitudinal methods and/or qualitative efforts would greatly help further in the understanding of how employees can effectively cope with work-family conflict.

Index